PUBLICATION GUARANTEED

(WELL, ALMOST!)

PUBLICATION GUARANTEED

(WELL, ALMOST!)

A HELPING HAND FOR WRITERS

ESTHER CHILTON

PUBLICATION GUARANTEED (WELL, ALMOST!)

INTRODUCTION

Okay, so this book is called 'Publication Guaranteed (well, almost!)'. Now, I would love to tell you I could guarantee you'll be a published writer, but that's why the 'well, almost' has been added. There are no guarantees, but if you follow the suggestions in this book, you'll be giving yourself every chance at becoming a published writer.

When I was a teenager, I won a writing competition. *This is it*, I thought, *I'm going to be a famous writer*. I wrote story after story and sent them all off. They were all rejected. So I gave up my dream and turned to the world of banking instead. I hated it. Nonetheless, it was a job. It paid the bills. My writing certainly wasn't going to.

A few years later, I had an injury to my back and was no longer able to work in the bank. I saw an advert for *The Writers Bureau* creative writing course, signed up and have never looked back. I soon realised why my stories hadn't been accepted for publication. I had a lot to learn – market research, analysing your market, targeting the right publication, tone, style, word count, editing and more. It sounds a bit daunting, but it's not. Just take it step-by-step.

Little by little, I began to get it right and have readers' letters, fillers, articles and short stories published. You can, too. And I'm here to help you. Inside this book, you'll find lots of advice, tips, examples and writing exercises to take you on your path to publication.

Good luck!

How Do I Start?

You've already made a great start – you've bought this book! And you clearly want to be a published writer. Perhaps you're taking a course but haven't had anything published yet. Or maybe you're doing it all on your own and you're not sure what to do next. Whatever your path, don't worry; we'll get there together.

What do I need?

- **A laptop or computer.** Not long ago, editors accepted handwritten readers' letters and articles. Those days are now over and editors expect everything sent to them to be typed.

- **Internet access and email.** A lot of editors and publishers now accept short stories, competition entries, novel submissions, etc by email.

- **Microsoft Word.** Some publications and competitions still prefer work to be sent as a Word-compatible file (.doc or .docx or .rtf).

- **Printer and plain computer paper.** A small number of editors and publishers still prefer your work to be sent by post, so if that's the case, you'll need to print it out and send it.

- **Stationery.** Notebooks are useful for jotting down ideas, planning, etc. You'll also need stamps, pens, paperclips to secure your pages together (editors/publishers prefer this to stapling them), Post-its, etc.

- **Camera.** This is useful for photos to accompany readers' letters and articles.

Where do I work?

That's up to you. Some writers have an office, with plenty of space around it, while others have to clear a cluttered dining table and squeeze their laptop onto that. I've written in the back of my car in a dingy car park, at a picnic table at a farm park with children screaming in my ear and while sat in the dentist's waiting room. It's not ideal, but if you want to write, you'll write!

Be organised

It's a good idea to set up a record of the work you've sent out, otherwise you'll soon forget what you've sent, when and who to. You can keep records in a notebook or on your computer. They don't need to be elaborate. You could set it out in columns with headings such as:

Title – Date Sent – Publication – Accepted/Rejected Date – Paid? – Amount Received

These are just ideas – you may well come up with your own.

Expenses

You'll also need to record your expenses. For example, stamps, ink cartridges, pens, etc. Always keep your receipts. You can offset expenses against your earnings from writing.

The reason you need to do all this is because anything you earn from your writing has the potential to be taxable. So, you'll need to register with HM Revenue and Customs as self-employed. This is the case whether you're already working for an employer on a full- or part-time basis, or if you're not working at all. It also means you'll need to submit a tax return each year. For more information about this, visit **www.hmrc.gov.uk**. Or, if your tax affairs look likely to be complicated, consult an accountant.

Start small

What do you want from your writing? To be a famous novelist? Screenwriter? Freelance writer penning articles and short stories? Great. It's fantastic to have goals. You might be lucky and have work accepted straight away, though you'll be in the minority if you do. So, it's good to start small.

The first piece of work I had published was a reader's letter. It was only 50 words in length, but it was published writing. I built on that by sending out another and another. It wasn't long before I was having several letters a month published. It gave me confidence. Yes, it was only a reader's letter, but magazines and newspapers receive hundreds of letters every week and can only publish a few. If your letter is chosen, it means it's been picked over lots of others and that you're writing exactly what the editor is looking for. I'd done this by researching the readers' letters market very carefully. We'll come on to market research and look at it in more depth in the next chapter.

After readers' letters, I moved on to fillers (an explanation about what fillers are can be found in the relevant chapter), then article writing and short story writing. I used the same principles I'd used for readers' letters for other types of writing, building up my skills and confidence all the while. Little by little I got there and so will you.

Rejection

Rejection is part and parcel of a writer's life. I could paper my whole house with the rejection letters I've had over the years! Yes, it stings when you receive a rejection. Your first thought is likely to be that the precious piece of work you've spent hours lovingly nurturing isn't good enough. However, that rejection could be for all sorts of reasons. For example, the editor thought your article was superbly written, but because they've recently accepted an article on the same topic you've written about, they can't publish another one. Or the editor might have loved the filler you've sent for a specific slot, only they're changing that slot.

On the other hand, perhaps it isn't quite right. It happens to us all. One of my writer friends has had thousands of articles published and his success rate is about 50%. You're not going to get it right every time. But the more time you spend agonising over the rejected piece, the less time you have in writing something else. Move on to the next piece of writing – you may get that spot on. Don't linger too long on rejection. Use it to spur you on to acceptance.

Join a writers' group

Writers' groups are great for finding like-minded people. You'll find you're not alone in being uncertain and unsure about your work, so they're ideal for giving you plenty of encouragement and support. They're also a good way of motivating you to write and also for inspiring you to become a better writer.

Writers' groups contain writers of various genres and levels of skill. They'll be happy to share their knowledge and contacts, which can be invaluable.

Subscribe to a writing magazine

There are several writing magazines available in the shops. They're packed full of advice on all aspects of writing, from how to write dialogue and crafting characters, to structuring articles and inspirational interviews with authors, to useful information for beginners. Not only do they offer lots of helpful tips, they make you feel you're not alone and that you're part of a writing community.

Writing is a learning curve. I've been a freelance writer for over twenty years and I still subscribe to a writing magazine. I read it from cover to cover and there's never an issue I don't learn from, be it a new idea or way of writing.

Attend a writing festival

Writing festivals take place in cities and towns throughout the country. Many of them feature author talks and workshops. Go along to an author talk and you'll find yourself inspired to work on your own writing. Take part in a workshop and not only will you have lots of fun, you'll learn new skills and come out feeling motivated to build on those newfound skills.

They're also a great way of networking and meeting other writers. You'll find yourself connecting with authors, book bloggers, editors, publishers and lots of others in the writing world. I've made many a new writing friend this way, too – friends I now meet up with at other writing festivals and have contact with in between. We support and inspire each other in our writing.

Finally, don't forget to keep on writing!

If you want to become a published writer on a regular basis, you'll need to write on a regular basis. If you write an article and wait to hear back from the editor before working on your next piece of work, there's a chance you'll be in for a long wait. Editors are very busy and often take a few weeks to come to a decision. What happens if the editor comes back and says no? All that time you've been waiting could have been spent writing other pieces and sending them out. The more you write and send out, the greater your chances of having work accepted.

But it will take you a while to find your feet and to get into the habit of writing regularly. Take it a step at a time.

MARKET RESEARCH

So, you're all set and ready to start writing. Wrong! Before you can start working on a reader's letter, article or short story, you need to research the market. Researching the publication you want to write for is so important. It's no good writing a story or article and sending it off to a publication you haven't even looked at. How do you know what type of article they accept? The word length of the stories they publish? You've written a reader's letter? Great, but do they even publish readers' letters?

All publications differ in terms of the type of story or article they're looking for, the length of work they accept, the readership they're appealing to and so on. Writing is a highly competitive field as it is. Editors are often sent hundreds of readers' letters every week, numerous ideas for articles, etc. If you don't take the time to analyse your market, you greatly reduce your chances of acceptance.

But how do I begin? What if I don't know the publication I want to write for?

Don't worry; you're not alone. It can seem daunting to even know where to start. There are lots of ways of researching your market:

National newsagents

For print magazines/newspapers, it's useful to have an actual copy of the publication. This way, you can analyse the magazine/newspaper from cover to cover and get a good insight into what the editor is looking for (I'll take you through this in more depth later). *WHSmith* and other national newsagents sell all sorts of newspapers and magazines covering a wide range of topics including hobbies, travel, history, nostalgia and much more. Additionally, it can be surprising what your local newsagent stocks.

If ever I want to find a new publication to try, I find it useful to take a trip to a newsagent's. I'll take my time, looking along the shelves. Sometimes I have no idea what I'm looking for, so I'll peruse the various sections. For example, there's one on pets. I like cats and have my own so I've found new pet/cat magazines to target this way. The women's weeklies offer lots of different opportunities so I'll often buy a couple of those to see what I can write for them. I write articles for magazines about various places around the country, too. While browsing the newsagent's shelves one day, I stumbled upon a couple of magazines that accept this type of piece.

I usually buy a few at a time and then go home and analyse them thoroughly, with the aim of writing at least one article/filler/letter for each publication.

Websites

Most print publications also have websites, which can provide more information about what to write. However, be careful of using websites as your sole means of research because not all of them cover every section included in the magazines themselves. Nor do they always give you examples of the type of work featured in the print versions. Others have excellent websites where you can view previous issues and see detailed writers' guidelines. If a website doesn't give information concerning guidelines, most publications are happy to provide them on request either by post or e-mail.

Freebies

Look out for free magazines and papers. In some areas of the country, you'll receive a free local newspaper through your letterbox. There are also magazines you can pick up for free from hotels, banks, chemists and supermarkets. Lots of these offer opportunities to writers and this type of publication seems to be on the increase.

Top tip

Make sure your research is up-to-date. Magazines and newspapers are changing all the time so if you have an older copy, the information may not be current. Similarly, websites featuring writers' guidelines are sometimes several years old and requirements have changed.

Lists of fiction markets can easily be printed out from the Internet, giving you an idea of which to target. But fiction is a dwindling market and many of these lists haven't been updated for a good while. Therefore, some of the publications listed no longer publish fiction or a few listed could even have folded.

You may have a copy of a women's weekly that's a year old. New slots are popping up every week while others fall by the wayside so you could target a slot no longer there.

It's fine to use these research tools, but use them alongside a recent copy of the publication and e-mail the editor for current guidelines.

The Internet

As well as using the Internet to see if a magazine you want to write for has writers' guidelines or any other useful information, you can also use it to find markets to write for. If you like writing about travel, type 'travel magazines' into your search engine. All sorts of information comes up – from actual magazines and their websites, to sites listing the top travel magazines to write for. You'll also see travel magazines for countries the world over, which means you can write for international markets, too.

Online publications

Moving away from print publications, there are lots of online publications and ezines, offering more opportunities for writers. The same rules regarding research apply to these as for any other publication.

Writing magazines

I've already touched on these, but as well as being full of helpful guidance and advice for writers, there's usually market information in them. This can sometimes be in the form of an interview with the editor of a magazine and includes useful tips about writing for that publication. At the very least, you may discover a publication you didn't know about and you can now go and research it with a view to writing for it.

Writing Magazine (**https://www.writers-online.co.uk/**) and *Writers' Forum* (**https://writers-forum.com/**) are two of the best.

The Writers' and Artists' Yearbook

This reference book is published annually and is packed full of markets to send your writing to. There's a section on magazines and newspapers where you'll find plenty of information about possible publications to send your work to. But it's not just a book for writers of articles, fillers, readers' letters and short stories. There are also sections on finding a publisher for your novel or non-fiction book, as well as sections on poetry, television and radio, to name a few.

The Writers' and Artists' Yearbook contains lots of practical information on finance, tips on all sorts of aspects of writing and much more.

Nonetheless, whilst it's an invaluable tool, and there are other similar reference books out there, you will need to carry out further research alongside it. The book is usually over 800 pages in length, so to put it all together takes some time. Within that time, huge changes could have taken place. For example, from reading the reference guide, you've found a particular magazine you'd like to write for. Perhaps the guide includes information about a romance story of 1000 words, which is published in each issue. Fast forward to now and the magazine might no longer publish fiction at all. Or they've decided the maximum word limit for stories is 800 words. If you use the guide as your sole reference point, you could be wasting your time if you write a 1000-word story and send it off. Again, make sure your research is up-to-date and check what they're currently accepting.

Readly

Earlier on, I mentioned browsing through the newsagent's shelves and selecting several magazines to buy. Have you been mentally totting up how much that's going to cost? Magazines aren't cheap. That's why I'm selective. I take my time in deciding which ones to buy and I'll always try and write at least one piece of work for them so I'll (hopefully!) earn more than the cost of the magazine. But, there are other ways of accessing magazines and newspapers without taking a trip to the newsagent's or spending money on each magazine.

This is where *Readly* steps in. For a small monthly fee (at the time of writing, there's a special offer to start, together with a 'cancel at any time' policy), you can have access to thousands of magazines. The facility allows you to read the magazines as well as download and save them.

Go to **https://gb.readly.com/** and click on the GB flag. A list of countries where it's available will come up and you can select the one you want.

Now try this

Keen to find publications to write for? Before you head off to the newsagent's or start typing words into your search engine, it's useful to write down subjects that interest you. For example:

- Cars

- Knitting

- Gardening

- History

- Dogs

- Caravanning

- Ghost stories

This is just a short example, and do keep adding to your list, but if you have a list of your hobbies and interests, it'll at least give you an idea of the type of magazine you're looking for as you scan the newsagent's shelves, search the Internet, etc.

What next?

Hopefully you'll now have a pile of publications or downloaded publications you'd like to write something for. The next step is to analyse them.

> # Top tip
>
> If you can, it's a good idea to read a few issues of each publication. It allows you to get more of a feel for it and what the editor is looking for.

What to look for

Analysing your market involves looking at the publication as a whole. Say you want to write an article for a particular magazine, you'll need to study more than just the articles in the magazine. The following guide will take you through what to look for and why:

- **The first thing to check is what opportunities there are for writers.** Some magazines state they don't accept freelance submissions. Under the magazine's address and contact details, it'll say something along the lines of 'No unsolicited material accepted'. Others will say the magazine 'cannot accept responsibility for any unsolicited material'. This means they do accept unsolicited work; they just don't take responsibility if it goes missing. Nonetheless, even if the magazine states it doesn't accept unsolicited work, you can still send them a query letter/email outlining your idea and asking them if they'll consider accepting an article from you. They just prefer not to be sent full articles in the first instance. Writing a query letter/email will be covered later.

- **Make notes on the type of reader you're writing for.** How old do you think the average reader is? The articles and adverts can often help to give an indication of this. For example, if there are adverts for stair lifts and funeral plans, you're catering to an over 50s market. What do you think they enjoy doing? Where are they likely to work? Knowing the reader you're writing your article for will help you to write it with them in mind, meaning you're more likely to target the publication correctly.

- **Think about the publication's style and tone.** Is the wording easy to understand or is the language more erudite? Has it been written for the lay reader or does the reader need a certain level of knowledge?

What topics are covered in the articles/stories? This will help to give you ideas about what sorts of subjects the reader is interested in and it'll also give you ideas for what you can write about.

You should now be forming an image of your reader and the type of piece likely to be accepted.

I'll cover how to analyse readers' letters, fillers, articles and short stories in greater depth in each relevant chapter.

READERS' LETTERS

I'm going to start with readers' letters. *Why?* I hear you cry. *I want to write articles and short stories, not readers' letters.* As I mentioned earlier, it's good to start small. Readers' letters are a form of writing that's often dismissed. Here are some reasons why they shouldn't be ignored. Writing readers' letters:

- **Earns you money:** Did you know you can earn around £200 pounds a month from readers' letters? Whilst you can't live off the proceeds of readers' letters alone, you can earn between £25 - £50 a letter. It's easy to get into the habit of writing a handful a week as they're only very short (often less than 100 words). Write them well and you'll find yourself with a high success rate and cheques coming in.

- **Builds confidence:** There's nothing like that feeling of first having something published, no matter what it is. Whether you punch the air with joy, dance around the room or shout from the rooftops, it's exciting and makes you feel good. Having a few readers' letters published gives you confidence. I can write and my writing is good enough to be published. After I'd had several readers' letters in print, it gave me the confidence to try other types of writing. If I can write readers' letters and sell them, I can write fillers and articles.

- **Hones your writing skills:** As I've already mentioned, readers' letters are short. Some publications take longer letters. For example, nearly 200 words in length; others prefer much shorter letters. This means you don't have many words in which to get your point across. So letter writing is all about being succinct. Your letter also needs to catch the editor's eye to

15

be chosen, meaning it's a great way to practice short, sharp and to the point writing. You can carry this forward into other types of writing.

- **The fun factor:** Get into writing readers' letters and you'll soon find they're fun to write. You may well want to continue writing them even if you move on to writing articles, short stories and books, just because they're a welcome distraction and offer something a little bit different before you get back to your other writing. And, if you're struggling with writer's block or feeling bogged down in the depths of your novel, they can be just the tonic you need to get you back on track with your writing.

- **Quick and easy:** As many of the letters are short, they don't take long to write and so they won't take up a lot of your time.

Who publishes readers' letters?

The women's weeklies, arguably, offer the greatest opportunity for having a reader's letter published. Most of them have a page, or even two, devoted to letters. About half of them only pay for the star letter; the other half pay for each letter they use.

The national newspapers publish readers' letters. A lot of them don't pay, or pay for the star letter/offer a prize, say a weekend away. Local newspapers sometimes have a letters page, though you're unlikely to gain any payment or a prize.

General interest publications such as *Reader's Digest* have a couple of pages for letters. Payment is made per letter published.

You'll find letters pages in gardening magazines, TV magazines, magazines about all the different soap operas on TV, the women's monthlies, magazines related to nostalgia, sewing, cars, finance, pets, boating and so on. You may find money or vouchers are given for letters published, prizes related to the subject of the magazine or it may be simply the sheer joy of seeing your name and letter in the publication is all that's on offer. Regardless, it's publication. And having any letter published gives you something to build on.

Top Tip

Can you send your letter to more than one publication at a time? Surely it's a good idea to send it to several different publications at once? Wouldn't you stand a better chance of being accepted that way? You might, but if you've sent it to three different publications and all three want to use your letter, you'll have to turn two down. Magazines and newspapers want exclusive letters, not ones that have already been published. And if you start turning editors down, they won't be very happy and will be less likely to publish future writing from you. This goes for fillers, articles, short stories and competition entries, too.

Analysing readers' letters

It's important to study the letters pages before you write your own. Make notes on the following:

Type of letters

What are the letters about? If you read a few copies of the magazine/newspaper you're thinking of writing a letter for, you'll get a feel for the sort of letter they publish. For example, a local newspaper is likely to publish letters about reports in a previous issue of the paper, things happening around the area, events, problems around the locality, etc.

For TV magazines, all the letters relate to TV programmes recently aired.

In some of the women's weeklies, you'll find letters about articles published in the last couple of issues, letters about overcoming something difficult, letters about pets, children, family and friends, funny anecdotes and so on.

A magazine on cookery may publish letters about readers putting recipes from a previous issue into practice. Or you might see a letter about how a reader discovered the magazine and how useful they've found it.

Writing magazines are full of letters sharing readers' experiences of writing. There will also be letters about articles the magazine has published and letters making suggestions about what the magazine could cover or what readers like and don't like.

Whichever publication you're going to write for, you need to know what type of letter they use. For example, if you send a letter to a magazine about something funny that happened to you and the magazine only publishes letters about previous articles they've featured, your letter won't be used.

Top Tip

If your letter is about an article/report previously printed in your target publication, make sure you send it out as soon as you can after the magazine/newspaper has been published. If you leave it for a few weeks/months, the publication will have moved on to other articles and reports printed more recently and be publishing letters about those.

Word length

How many words does each letter use? Every letter will vary slightly: some publications use letters ranging in word length from as little as 20 words, going up to 80. Others, such as the national broadsheets, will publish much longer letters of over 100 words.

It's important to know how long your letter needs to be. For example, if you write a letter of 150 words to one of the women's weeklies and the maximum number of words they use in a letter is 60, they won't be able to publish your letter, even if they like the content, because it's too long. Yes, there's the possibility they'll edit it, but if that happens the intended message in the letter might be lost. Besides, editors are busy people and it's far easier for them to publish a letter that's the right length.

Sentence and paragraph length

This follows on from the subject of word count. Take a look at the average number of words in each sentence. As with the word count, if the publication clearly uses letters with only a small number of words in each sentence, follow suit and don't make your sentences long and wordy.

Are the letters published structured into paragraphs? If the letters are very short, they probably won't be, but for longer letters they're likely to be. Study the example of the letters printed and do the same.

Top Tip

While it's fun to use a fancy font, or add in cute images, don't. Editors and editorial staff are inundated with letters and just want to see the content of your letter. Keep it simple. Times New Roman or Arial are preferred by editors and a font size of 12.

Style and tone

You'll need to get this aspect right. For example, if you're writing for a magazine that's more upmarket and knowledgeable, you'll need to reflect this in the way you write your letter and the language you use. Conversely, if your target market is a popular magazine, don't use language of a technical nature. The more you follow the lead of the letters the publication uses, the more chance you have of having your own published.

Top Tip

You may be wondering how you'll know if your letter is going to be published. Does someone from the publication let you know? Sometimes they do, but not always. It is a nuisance, but it's often simply a case of checking the publication to see if it's in there, which isn't always easy to do – you don't want to have to stand in the newsagent's every week, trawling through magazines. Again, Readly can help with this as you can easily check if you've had a letter published.

How do I set my letter out?

It depends how you send it. Before the Internet and social media, the only way you could send a reader's letter was by post. Most publications will still accept letters by post. If you prefer to send your letters that way, do. Many publications have Facebook pages and Twitter and Instagram accounts, which enable you to comment. Some of them publish several of these on their letters pages. But the most common way to send your letter, at the time of writing, is by email.

The publication should give an email address for your letters to be sent to. In the subject line, I usually keep it simple and write 'Letter', or 'Letter and photo' if I'm including a photo. Then, in the body of the email, write your letter. It always looks good if you address your letter to the editor (unless a different person is specified) and name them; it shows you've taken the time to find out their name and have an interest in their publication. Once you have written your letter, sign it off with 'Best wishes' or Kind Regards', followed by your name, address, email address and phone number. Always remember to add in your contact details. Otherwise, how will they know where to send your cheque/prize? A few of the women's weeklies also like your age to be included. Before you send your letter, always check if there's anything else they'd like you to add. Here's an example of how to send a letter to a writing magazine by email:

To: letters@writinglife.com

Subject: Letter

Dear (add the editor's name – just their first name is fine),

We all know editors are very busy people (yourself included, of course), so after sending out an article idea, how soon do we chase it up? Two weeks later? A month? Or should we just send it off and move on to the next writing project, safe in the knowledge that if the editor wants our work, they'll get back in touch with us (hopefully soon)?

I once sent an article to a particular magazine as they accepted unsolicited manuscripts. I didn't hear back so I sent a polite follow-up letter a short while later. When I didn't hear back again, I presumed the editor wasn't interested and so I worked on other pieces of writing for other magazines.

Thirteen years later, I received a letter in the post thanking me for my wonderful article and informing me it was going to be featured in the magazine. It's a shame it took him thirteen years to realise how wonderful my article was, but it was an unexpected sale and the pay was rather more than it was thirteen years ago.

I wonder if other readers can top that wait!

Kind Regards,

Esther Chilton
1 Writers Row
Writing Land
WR1 1TR

estherchilton@writingmail.com
01234 56789

> # Top Tip
>
> Your letter may be seasonal or related to a specific date coming up. Say your letter is about Christmas. Make sure you send your letter off in plenty of time – don't leave it to the week before Christmas. Weekly magazines plan several weeks ahead and monthly magazines at least a couple of months ahead.

Now try this

From your market research, you should have found some publications, which accept readers' letters. Write one and send it off. Then write another. If you can, set yourself a target of writing five a week. The more you write, the greater chance you have of having a letter published. Five may seem a lot so build up to it. And remember – many of the publications only require a letter of a few words.

For examples of published readers' letters, see page 113.

FILLERS

Fillers are often overlooked as writing opportunities, with the majority of writers concentrating on articles, short stories and novels/non-fiction books. But filler pieces are fun, easy to write, often only a few paragraphs in length and there are a lot of magazines crying out for them.

What exactly is a filler?

Fillers cover all sorts of subjects and can range in length from several words and a photo, up to a 500-word mini-article. It might be a quiz, or a mini interview. Short tips pieces and facts pieces come under the filler umbrella.

Who publishes fillers?

You'll find possible markets everywhere! The best market is arguably the women's weeklies. Many of them have pages devoted to photos with a short, quirky caption. They also invite tips for around the home, as well as photos of your children/grandchildren and pets. Some have slots for a rant over something that's annoying you, while others have a page inviting readers to write in with a beauty question.

Other markets are general interest publications. Typical slots found are funny true-life anecdotes, short travel pieces, trips down memory lane, joke slots and funny signs.

Gardening magazines offer filler opportunities such as gardening tips and short pieces on readers' gardens.

Cookery magazines, newspapers and general interest publications often have filler slots inviting favourite or unusual recipes.

Local and national newspapers publish reviews. For example, restaurant, book and theatre reviews. Some accept them from freelancers.

The above are just a few of the common filler opportunities you'll find.

Top Tip

Fillers slots come and go all the time so do keep looking out for new opportunities.

How do I find markets for fillers?

There are several ways you can go about it:

You can use a resource tool like *Writing Magazine* (mentioned earlier on - found in a larger newsagent's). They devote several pages to markets for writers and often include details of publications inviting fillers. But you'll also need to get a copy of the publication so you can see the type of filler they're looking for and so you can get a feel for the publication as a whole.

I've found filler slots by simply buying newspapers and magazines and analysing them. So perusing the shelves of a newsagent's can lead to the discovery of filler opportunities.

You can use the Internet, though it's a bit hit and miss. Type 'filler opportunities for writers' or 'publications accepting fillers' into your search engine and a few blog posts/comments on websites about them come up but not really any concrete publications to write fillers for. It's often a matter of having a play around with the words before you hit on something useful.

Analysing fillers:

As with readers' letters, it's crucial to analyse the type of fillers a publication uses if you want yours to be accepted. The analysis involved is similar to that for readers' letters:

Type of filler

What sort of filler does the publication print? Recipes? Reviews? Tips pieces? You may read a publication and think they could benefit from a funny anecdote slot, but editors have specific slots they want filled. If you send in something they don't publish, it's unlikely to be accepted. But by all means, send in a reader's letter suggesting it and get the editor thinking about it for the future.

Word length

Pay careful attention to the word length and write yours to fit in with the set length, if specified, or average word length of the fillers used, if not.

Sentence and paragraph length

Make sure your filler is structured in the same way as the fillers the magazine uses. For example, if you're writing a filler of 400 words, you'll need to break it down into paragraphs.

Style and tone

Read the publication carefully to get a feel for the language and voice that needs to come through in your writing to reach the reader. Chatty? Instructional? Humorous?

Top Tip

Fillers are an ideal way for new writers to break into a market, but many established writers enjoy them, too, as they fit in perfectly with bigger projects. So, once you start having work regularly published, you might well continue writing the odd filler or two.

A lot of the publications, which accept fillers, provide guidelines. Often an email/letter with a couple of lines, leading into the filler, is all that's necessary, together with your contact details. For a longer filler, the publication may prefer the work to be sent as an attachment.

How do I set my filler out?

For very short fillers for the women's weeklies, it's usual to send them as you would a reader's letter. Most publications will make it clear. If you're really not sure, either email or phone the publication to check. They don't mind and are usually very helpful. On the next page is an example of how to send a tip by email to a women's weekly. A photo of the tip should also be sent. The best way to send the photo is as an attachment.

To: womanswondermagazine@womansmedia.com

Subject: Your bright ideas tip

Dear (add editor's name or the relevant person if named),

I love reading the tips in Woman's Wonder Magazine. I thought I'd share mine with readers:

I started using dental picks to clean between my teeth but found I was still suffering with staining in between the teeth (I drink too much tea!). So I tried dipping the dental stick in toothpaste and then using it to clean in between my teeth. It's worked a treat and I now have sparkling gnashers!

Kind Regards,

Esther Chilton
1 Writers Row
Writing Land
WR1 1TR

estherchilton@writingmail.com
01234 56789

Top Tip

Even with longer fillers i.e. those around the 500-word mark, you don't generally need to send a query first – just send the full piece.

Now try this

As you'll have seen from the examples, fillers can be very short and on a wide variety of topics. To build up your confidence, write a few tips and/or funny anecdotes first and send them off. Then, when you feel ready, write a longer piece. But keep working on the short fillers, too. They can pay well and they're good practice. Have some published and you'll be keen to move on to article writing.

For examples of published fillers, see page 115.

ARTICLES

So, you've written a few readers' letters and fillers and feel ready to move on to the next level? Great. It's time to get stuck into article writing. And the good news is, newspapers and magazines are full of articles meaning there are lots of opportunities for you to get your articles published.

Through your market research into readers' letters and fillers, you'll have hopefully already come across several publications you feel you can write an article for. If you're not sure what to write about, here are some topics published articles often cover:

- True-life, personal stories

- Food

- Health

- Shopping

- Fashion

- Family

- Finance

- Pets

- Hobbies

- Travel

- Education

- Relationships

- Sex

- Sport

- Beauty

- Nostalgia

- Computers

- Photography

- Music

- Gardening

- History

- The countryside

- Royalty

- Transport

The list goes on!

You'll find more ways of coming up with ideas for articles in the next chapter.

Analysing articles

As you'll no doubt be realising by now, market research is vital. You might think a pet magazine would like an article on guinea pigs so you write a brilliantly entertaining and informative article for them, only to get a rejection letter back, stating they don't feature small pets in the magazine. It's essential to know what the magazine covers.

It's also important to know how they like their articles structured. For example, you may have interviewed a local businessman for a magazine, which focuses on a certain industry. The magazine might publish interviews but like their interviews in a Q&A style (where the questions asked are written out in full, followed by the answers underneath) and you've written the interview out as a proper article, interspersed with the interviewee's own words. The editor likes your article but is so busy they don't have time to ask you to rewrite it and so they move on to another interview someone has sent in, which has been written up in the correct way.

I've covered analysing your market as a whole already (go back to the chapter on market research and read through 'what to look for' again as a reminder) as well as for readers' letters and fillers. Here are some more tips on how to analyse articles in the publication you want to write for:

Article length

As with readers' letters and fillers, it's important to adhere to the word length of the articles the publication uses. There may be writers' guidelines online or you could send a quick email or make a call to check. If not, you'll need to count the words. It is a bit of a pain, but if you count the words in a few articles, you'll soon be able to judge the word length and get a feel for the number of words per article.

Sentence and paragraph length

Again, you'll need to study this carefully. It does vary. For example, you'll likely see shorter sentences and paragraphs in a women's weekly than you will in one of the broadsheet newspapers. Always follow the lead of your target publication.

Title

This can vary from publication to publication. Some magazines and newspapers have headings that are self-explanatory. For example, 'Five facts about cats you didn't know', so you're already aware what the article is going to be about. Others are short and to the point, some are descriptive, while others tease and hook the reader's interest into finding out more. For example, 'Go home, soldier!' There are lots of publications that use a mixture.

Lead-in

Most articles have an introductory paragraph, explaining what the articles are about. Here is an example:

As is the case with many market towns around the country, Newbury, located in West Berkshire, and an hour's train journey from London, has seen rapid change over the years. But along the way, Newbury has many a unique and interesting tale to tell.

From the above, you know the article is going to be about Newbury's heritage, together with interesting stories about the town.

Others draw the reader in:

I've always had a thing about the cupboard under the stairs. You would think, too many decades on from my childhood than I care to remember, it wouldn't still send shivers up my spine every time I opened it.

Now you're wondering why the writer has 'a thing' about the cupboard under the stairs and so you're intrigued to read on.

Top Tip

When you're working on your own article, however you lead into it, don't make it too long. A big block of words at the beginning of your article is off-putting.

Main body

How are the articles structured? With eye-catching sub-headings? Bullet-point lists? Or is the article one flowing piece? How many facts/main points are included in the article? How does the writer ensure the points follow on from one to the other?

Top Tip

Balance is key. Don't feel as if you need to get everything out in the first few paragraphs. Spread it out over the course of the article. Nor should you concentrate your article on one single fact. If you do, you'll reach the word limit before you have time to cover the other facts.

Ending

Not all articles have a closing paragraph. For example, some interview pieces finish with the interviewee's last words. Tips pieces, such as 'Five Top Tips for Winter Gardens', sometimes finish with the final tip. But most articles have a short paragraph at the end, just to round the article off. Let's take the article about Newbury. After taking the reader on a journey through Newbury over the years, it ends with a paragraph about present-day Newbury:

Today, Newbury is a flourishing town, home to Vodafone's British headquarters, drawing people to the area. As with many towns, it's seen change in the high street, but the retail park to the south and Parkway Shopping Centre assure Newbury's commercial future. People still come from far and wide for its annual country show and the recent opening of the control tower at Greenham Common has raised interest in the town.

As for the article about the cupboard under the stairs, which was about a fear of spiders and how courage was plucked up to give the cupboard a good spring clean, it ended with the following:

Curtains, lampshades and shoes that had been in there so long they were now back in fashion, a bread maker, toaster – things I never knew I had. It was like going on a shopping spree without spending any money. I hadn't had so much fun in ages. Though, I think it would be rather fun to wait another ten years before cleaning the cupboard out again. Who knows what I might find next time?

But what if they don't take work from freelancers?

As I've touched on before, not all publications accept work from freelancers. If you're not sure, you can always check with them, by email or by phone. Or you can send them a query letter/email, outlining your article and asking them if they would be interested in seeing the full piece.

How do I write a query letter/email?

There are some important points to include in your query letter/email:

- **Always address the editor by name.** It looks more professional than 'Dear Sir/Madam' and shows you have taken the time to find it out.

- **Open with a short window into the subject.** Grab the editor's interest and follow the style used in the publication's printed articles.

- **Include details of your proposed title and word count.** The editor will be drawn in to finding out more if they like your title. It's also useful for them to know how long your article is going to be so they can work out if there's space for it.

- **Explain why your article should be considered.** Give the editor a reason why readers of their publication would find an article on the subject you're writing about of interest.

- **Explain why you are the person to write this article.** Do you have expertise in this area?

- **If you have had writing published, mention it.** It helps the editor know you have a track record.

- **Tell the editor a little bit about yourself – your job, or if writing is a hobby.** The editor always likes to know a little bit about who's writing for them.

- **Photos.** If you are providing photos to accompany your article, mention them.

- **Thank you.** Finish the pitch by thanking them for their time.

- **Contact information.** Always include your contact details so the editor can get hold of you if they need to discuss anything.

Here's an example of a query email. It resulted in a commission. The pitch was sent to a writing magazine:

To: freelancewriters@writing.com

Subject: Article pitch

Dear (add the editor's name),

With many writing competitions costing up to £8 or more to enter, is it really worth it? Enter three or four a month and you could find yourself spending £30 or so, with nothing to show for it. Even if you're named as a winner or runner-up, does it lead anywhere? As a writing tutor, many of my students complain they can't afford to keep entering competitions and even if they do, they don't feel they'll get anywhere or it'll do anything for them.

'I'm A Winner!' is a 1500-word article, featuring interviews with three writers whose lives have changed thanks to winning writing competitions. The article will highlight the competitions the writers entered, what the competition wins did for them and exactly how their lives have changed, including the doors it has opened for them. There will also be plenty of advice and tips on entering competitions from the writers.

I feel readers of your magazine will enjoy an article on this subject, and find it useful, as some of them may think about entering your competitions and others but don't actually get round to entering or think it's not worth it. For those that do enter, it will reinforce how worthwhile they are and what a difference a win can make.

As a winner of Writing Magazine and Writers' News competitions, I know first-hand how winning a writing competition can transform a writer's life. It certainly did mine. First of all, it gave me confidence; I realised I *could* write and if my writing was good enough to win such well-known competitions, then it was good enough to send out to editors.

Since winning Writing Magazine and Writers' News competitions, as well as becoming a writing tutor, I have had articles and short stories published in a variety of newspapers and magazines, ranging from The Guardian, to The People's Friend, to Collect It, to several writing magazines. I have also entered into the world of copywriting, undertaking work for Vodafone and national charity, Cats Protection. I run my own copyediting business and love helping others to achieve their writing dreams.

I hope you like the idea. Thank you for your time.

Kind Regards,

Esther Chilton
1 Writers Row
Writing Land
WR1 1TR

estherchilton@writingmail.com
01234 56789

Top Tip

Not all publications require photos to go with their articles. For example, the full article, 'I'm A Winner', in relation to the pitch to a writing magazine, didn't need illustrations, but there are lots that do. You'll be able to get a feel for which do and which don't from the magazine itself. Sometimes you'll see a photo credit by the side of the photo. If you're not sure, always check with the editor. If you can provide high quality photos if they're required, it'll enhance your chances of a sale.

What next?

You've sent your pitch off and received a positive response. Or perhaps the magazine doesn't need a pitch and accepts freelance work. Great! Get writing your article.

How do I set my article out?

On the first page of your manuscript, you should write your name, address, email address, phone number and the date in the top left-hand corner. In the top right-hand corner, you write part of your article title. For example, for an article called 'Bombast and Beauty', you would write 'Bombast 1'. Next, in the centre, you write your title and byline about a third of the way down the page.

On the next page, you don't need to write out your contact details again, but you do need to write the catchline i.e. 'Bombast'. You should also add in your surname and the next page number and so on for each subsequent page.

At the bottom of each page, write 'mf…' to indicate, literally, that 'more follows' i.e. more of the article is to come. On the last page you write 'END' so the editor knows your article has finished.

Top Tip

Many magazines and newspapers still prefer you to send your work in double spacing. If they specify this, then follow their guide. If you're not sure how to double space your text, the computer can do it for you. Go to the 'Help' tab and you'll be able to find out how you do this under 'Format text'. Also ensure you leave a good margin (about an inch and a half) at the bottom of your first page and at the top and bottom of the subsequent pages. If you don't indent your paragraphs (as I haven't in this book), you need to leave an extra line space in between each paragraph.

The following article, 'Bombast and Beauty', on the next page, was written for a writing magazine. It's written in the correct format i.e. in double spacing, with a catchline, etc.

1 Writers Row
Writing Land
WR1 1TR
Tel: 01234 56789
Email: estherchilton@writingmail.com

Bombast and Beauty

By Esther Chilton

As writers, we're often told flowery, ornate language is a thing of the past. But it seems in the case of beauty products, the more exaggerated and elaborate the better.

Here's a tongue-in-cheek look at some of the slogans and descriptions, which can be found at the beauty counter:

One Eau de Toilette spray can boast of the following description, 'Seductively spicy coriander and addictive fig surrounded by smouldering leather patchouli'. On its own, you've probably never thought of coriander as seductive. Neither is fig known as being particularly addictive. Chocolate, maybe. But for that matter, does the patchouli plant actually smoulder? Nonetheless, you have to admit, in using this sensuous description, it does rather conjure up the image of Colin Firth in 'Pride and Prejudice', which can't be a bad thing.

mf…

Chilton – Bombast 2

Some fragrances have 'feelings' attached to them. For example, 'Exhilarating, sexy, alive'. Is that in contrast to dead? And does that apply to the fragrance or you?

Another 'feeling' associated with a fragrance is, 'Radiant, rare, intriguing'. But surely if it's available in hundreds of stores nationwide, it can't be that rare. Though, from the price tag, perhaps you could be forgiven for thinking so. What's more, do you really want its delectable scent to make you feel rare, too, like a one-eyed, one-toed, triple-horned sloth or some such creature? The word 'intrigue' is also an interesting one. Can a perfume truly transform you from an unexciting, green cardigan and beige trouser wearing bore into a person who's mysterious and fascinating?

As well as 'feelings', some products actually seem to have a mind of their own. On using one mascara, apparently, 'Lashes seem to multiply, magnify, grow to extremes'. So if you see anyone with two-foot long lashes, you know what they've been using.

Another exercise in alliteration can be found with, 'Constant comfort for body'. This could be taken to mean your body is so awful it needs comforting continually.

mf…

Still on the subject of alliteration comes, 'Dramatically different moisturising gel'. Now, surely you're expecting something surprising here – perhaps a gel that does a little song and dance? And what about a product that's, 'So much more than a body lotion'? At the very least you'd want it to double up as a washing up liquid.

This light read finishes full circle and takes you back to a product for the male counterpart and a, 'Creamy bath and shower gel for real men'. Presumably this is in opposition to creamy bath and shower gel for fake men.

You can probably think up numerous ones of your own far more distinctive and extraordinary than these. So if you're writing a passage, which calls for a little bit of creativity and purple prose, pick up your perfume and be inspired.

END

Top Tip

Always follow the house guidelines of the magazine. So, if the guidelines state single spacing is to be used, and a different font, follow their requirements. If none are stated, follow the format suggested for 'Bombast and Beauty'. This is the case whether you're sending your article by post or by email.

The cover sheet

If you're sending your work by email, you won't need a cover sheet as all the necessary information will be in your covering email. But, if you're sending your article by post, you'll need one. Paperclip it to your article. It looks professional and also gives the editor all the important details they need. On the next page, you'll find a cover sheet for 'Bombast and Beauty'. You don't have to stick to this layout; the most important thing is to ensure your cover letter contains the relevant information i.e. your name, address, telephone number and email address, the word count and title of the article, as well as the date. In the case of the word count, always round it up or down to the nearest ten, as it looks more professional. For example, if an article is 879 words in length, round it up to 880.

1 Writers Row
Writing Land
WR1 1TR
Tel: 01234 56789
Email: estherchilton@writingmail.com

1st December 2020

Bombast and Beauty

A 480-word article

By

Esther Chilton

The covering letter/email

If you're sending your article by post, you'll need a covering letter; if it's by email, you'll need a covering email. It's very similar to the query letter/email. On the next page, there's an example of a covering letter for 'Bombast and Beauty'.

1 Writers Row
Writing Land
WR1 1TR

Writing World Magazine
123 Writing World Lane
Writing Land
WL1 2OP

1st December 2020

Dear (add editor's name)

I'm pleased to enclose a 480-word article, 'Bombast and Beauty', which I would be grateful if you would consider for publication in 'Writing World' magazine.

The article takes a fun look at some of the over-the-top descriptions the beauty industry gives their products. I believe readers of 'Writing World' will find the article entertaining and enjoy looking at beauty products in a different light, as well as making up some of their own descriptions.

I am a freelance editor and writing tutor and have written for a range of publications, including several writing magazines.

I hope you enjoy the article and look forward to hearing from you shortly. I have enclosed an SAE, should you not be able to use the article.

Kind Regards,

Esther Chilton
Tel: 01234 56789
Email: estherchilton@writingmail.com

You'll see I've made reference to an SAE (self-addressed envelope). It's essential you send this with a postal submission, if you'd like your manuscript returned to you. It may be you're not too worried about receiving it back, as you can easily print out another copy. But, if your script is returned to you, you'll usually receive a rejection letter with it and at least you'll know it's been rejected. Editors are increasingly busy and often don't reply if they're not going to use your work. So, if you don't enclose an SAE, the editor may not get in touch with you at all and as they can take months to come to a decision about whether they're going to use your work, you're left wondering.

What do I need to send if I'm posting my article?

- Covering letter

- Cover sheet

- Article

- SAE (with the correct return postage)

What do I need to send if I'm emailing my article?

- Covering email

- Article (as an attachment, unless specified otherwise)

- Any photos to accompany the article (as attachments)

Now try this

As you'll have seen, 'Bombast and Beauty' is a very short article and could be classed as a filler. But, as I've mentioned before, it's good to start off small.

Some newspapers and magazines publish articles of 2000 words; this can seem daunting when you're just beginning to write articles. A good place to start is to write about yourself. You'll find examples of published articles towards the back of this book. Two of them are about personal experiences. One of the first articles I ever had published was about going on holiday with my mum and dad when I was in my twenties. It was for a women's weekly and no more than 600 words.

Another starting point is, as the saying goes, 'write about what you know'. Are you an expert in your job? Have you got a hobby you could write about? Pets? A holiday you've been on?

You'll find plenty more ideas for articles in the next chapter.

For examples of published articles, see page 118.

AMAZING ARTICLE IDEAS

Hopefully, after reading the previous chapter and analysing magazines and newspapers, your head is full of ideas for entertaining and informative articles. But we all get stuck for inspiration from time to time. Here are some ways to get the ideas flowing and a few writing exercises to try. Remember - before you start writing your article, be clear which publication you're targeting and always have it to hand so you write your own article up in a way that'll fit in with their style, tone and other requirements.

The publication itself

I've often found a good way to start my mind working is when I'm actually analysing the publication itself. I'll use the example of a cat magazine. You may want to write for a cat magazine but can't think of an original idea. Looking through the magazine in question, you come across a quirky and interesting article about cats and superstitions relating to them. This gets you thinking as you've heard an old saying about cats recently. With some research, you could build on this and turn it into a fun article about strange and amusing cat sayings over the years.

Alternatively, you're thinking of writing an article for a magazine whose focus is on collecting. Perhaps you collect trinket boxes but you find the magazine has recently featured an article on this subject. Don't set the magazine aside as a market. Instead, analyse it for ideas for other articles. A piece on someone who collects old bookmarks may feature a cricket scene. You have a relative who collects cricket memorabilia, including some rare and valuable pieces. This would make a highly interesting article for the magazine.

Writing exercise

When you next look through a magazine or newspaper, see if you can write down at least five ideas for articles. Keep an open mind and let the ideas come. They may not all be practical to use but two or three out of the five might.

_____

_____

_____

_____

_____

_____

_____

_____

_____

_____

_____

_____

Other magazines and newspapers

Even when you're not analysing a magazine or newspaper with a view to writing an article, you might read one for pleasure, a daily newspaper, say, or a magazine you've subscribed to for years. Articles, features, letters, etc can all trigger a wealth of ideas for articles of your own.

Writing exercise

Keep a notebook (whether it's a physical notebook, your iPad, phone, laptop, etc, it's up to you) handy when you're reading any publication. You never know when the ideas will come and if you don't write them down when you see them, it's easy to forget them.

_____

_____

_____

_____

_____

_____

_____

_____

_____

_____

PUBLICATION GUARANTEED (Well, almost!)

Your own experiences

Open up any of the women's weeklies and you'll see pages and pages of true-life stories. These range from stories about 'my operation', to overcoming an illness/divorce/death in the family, to doing something special, to an amusing pet story. If you did something a little different for a milestone event – a 50th birthday or a Golden Wedding Anniversary – you could write up your own story for one of the magazines. Similarly, a women's weekly would love to hear how you recovered from life threatening surgery and went on to have a baby, jump out of a plane or gain a well-earned degree. Your experience needn't be sensational. True, the magazines do feature many jaw-dropping stories, but they also publish lots of heart-warming ones.

There are plenty of other magazines that want to know about your experiences. For example, there are several cat and dog magazines, which invite owners' stories. Or if keeping chickens is more your thing, there's a number of smallholder magazines crying out for useful information and advice.

It's easy to overlook your experiences and to believe no one is likely to want to hear about them. Rest assured, they certainly do. For example, if you volunteer for a charity on a regular basis or were made redundant and have started your own business, one of the women's glossies is likely to want to hear about it.

Writing exercise

Write down five things that have happened to you – have you won any special awards? Have you helped someone achieve something? Have you or a member of your family overcome an illness? What about a dramatic career change? Did you hit your 60s and decide to learn a new skill? These are just five ideas I've come up with quickly and I'm sure you'll have lots of different experiences to list – ones you can turn into an article for a variety of publications.

PUBLICATION GUARANTEED (Well, almost!)

Hobbies

I mentioned writing about a hobby at the end of the last chapter. There's probably a magazine for every type of hobby, from stamp collecting, to music, to photography, to sailing, to cross stitch. Most of them have letters pages inviting readers to share their thoughts on the magazine and also anything on the subject they'd like to write about. Many also welcome material from freelance contributors. If you have some rare stamps or enjoy researching them, a stamp collecting magazine is a good target market. Or, if you make up your own cross stitch designs, why not send them to a publication specialising in the craft?

Writing exercise

Make a list of your hobbies – past and present. Even if you no longer indulge in your hobby, you may still be able to write about it or interview someone else who has the same hobby and write about them. Think about the different types of magazine you could send letters, fillers and articles about hobbies to - the women's weeklies, general interest publications, specialist hobby magazines, local and national newspapers and more.

Travel

This is another suggestion I ended the previous chapter with. All of us have travelled somewhere, be it to the exotic and mysterious land of the Pharaohs or the slightly less exotic and not quite so mysterious local market. Travel writing isn't all about beautiful, glamorous locations. A lot of travel magazines are looking for less well-known destinations or somewhere known as a tourist trap from a different angle. For example, an article about a famous ski resort but take out the skiing. What else is there for the tourist to do? Or a piece about Florida's other side - without the famous theme parks and usual attractions.

Some of the women's weeklies want to know about a favourite place, whether it's far away or just down the road. Others invite pieces on your hometown.

Open many a publication and you'll find travel somewhere inside, from national newspapers, to magazines for the over 50s, to magazines on travel and health, amongst others. So you'll have plenty of opportunities to write about travel.

Writing exercise

Think about three holidays you've been on. How could you give them a bit of a twist and write from a different angle? Then think about three places you've visited in your home country. For example, a local museum, a day trip to the seaside, or a shopping spree somewhere. Could you write a reader's letter, filler or full article about them?

When you go anywhere, always take a camera with you, even if it's just one on your phone. And make sure you snap away. You never know when you'll need a photo to accompany an article or reader's letter about a place you've visited.

Rant!

We all have pet-hates and things that make our blood boil. A lot of publications have specific slots inviting you to share your rant. For example, some of the women's weeklies and satirical publications. So whether it's politics, products or people, you can vent your anger on paper and get paid for it.

Writing exercise

Make a list of three things that annoy you and then justify why they annoy you. Keep it short and snappy as many of the slots inviting rants are less than 100 words.

_____

_____

_____

_____

_____

_____

_____

_____

_____

_____

PUBLICATION GUARANTEED (Well, almost!)

Anniversary/seasonal

Every day marks the anniversary of when someone famous died or when a unique invention first came to light. General interest magazines often feature this sort of piece. Additionally, depending on who the person is or what invention your article relates to, you may find a multitude of magazines interested in a piece of this nature. For example, a women's magazine, nostalgia publication or general interest magazine may be interested in an article on the 100th anniversary of the invention of the electric tumble dryer. Some research on this and the early dryers will make for a fascinating and entertaining read.

Similarly, seasonal articles. For example, Christmas. These are always popular. Though, articles such as 'Top 10 tips on looking your best for the office party' have been done time and time again and are often covered by a staff writer. See if you can find an unusual hook. For example, interview someone who works for a local charity that helps to feed the homeless on Christmas Day and ask them about what their day entails.

Writing exercise

Jot down the different seasons and then ideas about articles you could write about those times of the year. Think about unusual hooks to make yours catch the editor's eye. What about anniversaries? You'll need to carry out research for these. Nowadays it's very easy to do this via the Internet, with calendars of famous deaths, events and inventions readily available. Whatever you choose to write about, you must ensure your facts and dates are correct. Always double check them. If an editor finds out some of the information you've written is wrong, he's unlikely to accept your work again.

PUBLICATION GUARANTEED (Well, almost!)

Health

A lot of publications use articles by health experts. If you are one, great, but if you're not, it doesn't mean you can't write about it. Do you have acupuncture for health reasons? Would your therapist be willing to be interviewed? A health magazine might be interested in featuring an article in the autumn on acupuncture and ways to beat the common cold.

Words from an expert also add weight to your article. Do you see a chiropractor for your back? Advice from your chiropractor on backs and self-help or new, innovative treatments would be ideal for a variety of publications, including women's magazines, general interest and local magazines. Add some research on back pain and you're halfway to a sale.

If you're having homeopathic treatments, reflexology, physiotherapy - on and on the list goes - think about a new stance on it. For example, homeopathy and pets. There have been some amazing success stories in this area. Do some research and interview a therapist. It's interesting as well as providing a brilliant article.

Writing exercise

Make a list of all the different health problems you've had and the treatments. Next to them, note down ideas for turning these into articles. Or why not write about your health experience for one of the women's weeklies? They all have health pages. Even if there has been a serious side to the treatment, did something funny happen along the way? You could turn it into an anecdote for a general interest publication that has a slot for this type of filler, or is there a heart-warming outcome? It may not be long enough for a full article, but several of the women's weeklies feature this type of story on their letters pages.

PUBLICATION GUARANTEED (Well, almost!)

Life changes

We make lots of changes as we go through life. Are you going back to college to gain a degree or further your education? What's it like being a mature student? Do you have any tips on studying to share? General interest magazines, women's magazines, specialist publications and student magazines would be interested in your article. Or maybe you're changing careers in your 40s, 50s or 60s. What's it like? What sacrifices did you have to make? Business, local, general and women's magazines are ones to target here.

Writing exercise

List all the major changes you've made over the years. There will be more than you realise. Think about your experiences and the lessons you've learned along the way. Would you change things? If so, how would you go about it? You could write about each and every one of those changes. There'll be a market for each one.

Buying a new car, choosing a school for the kids, your relationship with your neighbours, phobias, hints and tips you've found round the house; the brainstorming just goes on. Hopefully these have helped spark a few ideas and maybe you'd like to add some of your own.

_____

_____

_____

_____

_____

_____

SHORT STORIES

For many, writing short stories and having them published is what it's all about – especially achieving publication in the women's weeklies. But, this is a very volatile market, with lots of the women's weeklies either no longer publishing fiction, or announcing they'll only accept stories from writers who've had stories published with them on a regular basis. So, for those trying to break into that market, the amount of opportunities have been reduced. Nonetheless, there are still women's weeklies that accept unsolicited stories. To keep abreast of the current situation (as it can change quickly), it's best to email them to check and to ask for current guidelines.

Which publications accept short stories?

All sorts of publications print short stories. These include:

- Women's weeklies – look out for the fiction special spin-offs, too

- Women's monthlies

- General interest publications

- National newspapers - magazine supplements

- Pet magazines

- Children's magazines

- Spiritual magazines

- Supernatural and ghost story magazines

- Small press markets

- Ezines

- Writing magazines

- Literary magazines

And more.

You'll find a lot of these magazines in your newsagent's, others online, through writers' resources such as *The Writers' and Artists' Yearbook* and *Writing Magazine*. There's also a very big competition scene, which I'll cover in a later chapter.

Start small – again

When I first started writing, I naively saw myself penning stories for all the women's weeklies and them being accepted every time! So I was very disappointed when they kept coming back with standard rejections letters. I've read my early attempts in recent times and I cringe. I can see exactly why they weren't accepted. The stories were very weak and didn't suit the market at all! When I'd collected enough rejections to paper one wall of a room in my house, I realised I was doing something very wrong.

So, I decided to start small (again, I'm sure you can see a pattern forming here) – literally – with the small presses. I subscribed to a couple and studied them carefully to get a feel for the type of stories they published. I then started to write my own and sent them in. Before too long, I was regularly having stories published. Not all paid and those that did, not very much. Nonetheless, it was a fantastic feeling to have my first short story published. It gave me confidence I could transfer this to the women's weeklies.

I did just that. But it wasn't easy. And, once again, researching your market and knowing the magazine and type of story the publication is looking for is key. Some writers make the mistake of thinking all women's weeklies are the same. They're not. For example, *The People's Friend* has a very distinctive style and feel to it. Their readers like a particular type of character and there are certain subjects which are taboo. Each magazine is unique. That isn't to say you can't tweak the stories and make them suitable for different publications. If one publication rejects one of your stories, you can send it to one of the others, but make sure you study the new publication you're intending to send it to and make any necessary changes so it fits in with the new publication's requirements.

Analysing short stories

Take a look back at the chapter on market research for a reminder of what to look for when you're studying magazines. Similar aspects to researching articles also apply to researching short stories – word length, style and tone, as well as the title. Here are some more points to make a note of when you've found a publication you'd like to write for and you're analysing its short stories:

What genre are the stories?

Does the publication use stories in a wide variety of genres? Or is their preference quite narrow? Perhaps they only use love stories or horror, crime and sci-fi. You'll need to keep to the genres they use, otherwise you'll find your stories rejected.

How does the story open?

With dialogue, plunging you straight into the story? Or with an action scene, gripping you and making you keen to read on and find out what happens? Sometimes the writer shocks, which makes the reader sit up and take notice. Here is an example of a story opening that does just that:

I didn't think looking down upon oneself when dead would be quite like this. In fact, I didn't believe in all that. Once you're dead, you're dead; aren't you?

I look at my face, so pale and my eyes, insignificant and lost amongst the dense drama of lashes. The slash across my mouth; Blood Red, the lipstick's called. God, what a state. How did I let it come to this?

Other times a story might start with humour and make the reader laugh, like the following:

Sam always knew his parents were strange. But when he saw them change colour and shape, he knew they were really strange. Up until that moment, that very moment when he had opened the door to their bedroom, he had thought they were like everyone else's parents. Everyone's parents were strange.

Parents belonged to another world. A world of completely and utterly no dress sense or hair sense. They liked watching old films. Films no one other than adults had ever heard of and listening to music from a bygone age, where all the singers wore dreadful clothes and hats.

Top Tip

Whatever you do, don't make the beginning of your story long and wordy. A rambling story opening about the weather or something incidental won't hook the editor's interest and have them wanting to read more. The rest of your story may be fantastic, but the editor's likely to have moved on to another story before they reach that point.

Main Body

Once a story has attracted the reader's attention with a gripping opening, it's crucial to keep it there. How does the writer do this? A good story will involve you, the reader, and ensure you stay involved. There needs to be at least one problem – something that happens to create tension and conflict, building up a sense of atmosphere all the while, propelling the reader, along with the characters, towards the story's climax.

Make notes on how much dialogue is used in the story. Dialogue is a very good tool for letting characters reveal themselves, for imparting information, injecting pace and pushing a story on.

Does the story have much description? In a short story, you won't have much time to linger on lengthy descriptions, but some description creates a sense of place so the reader can picture the scene in their mind.

How does the writer bring the characters to life? Through their words? Description? Their mannerisms and the things they do?

Which viewpoint is the story written in? A first-person viewpoint connects reader and character as the reader is taken on the story's journey with the character, seeing and feeling everything as they are. A third-person viewpoint allows more freedom and opens up the story so it can be seen through other characters' eyes not just the main protagonist's.

Top Tip

If you're describing a scene, think about using the different senses – sight, smell, sound, touch and taste. This helps to make the scene – and the story – more real for the reader.

Ending

Does the story leave you feeling satisfied? That's what a good story should do. The ending may have a surprise you weren't expecting or a twist. It might answer all the questions you had and so tie everything up. There are also open-ended story endings, which leave it up to the reader to decide.

Let's take the two story openings from earlier. The first story's main body gradually reveals who the character is and why she's found herself in her current situation. It ends with a surprise:

A flicker of movement. A finger. Mine. Now two. My hands wrap round the knife. I can't see myself any more, but I don't need to. I'm not done yet. But you are, darling husband. I'm coming for you.

In the other story, the main protagonist goes through a range of emotions as he finds out his parents are aliens from another planet and, by default, so is he. He feels shock, fear, uncertainty, excitement, happiness, love and finally, acceptance. The story leaves the reader with a warm glow and ties things up nicely:

To top it all, his mum and dad weren't half as bad as he had thought they were. In fact, he could safely say he had the coolest family on Earth.

Top Tip

Whatever you do, don't end your story 'It was all a dream'. This ending has been done numerous times over and now it's seen as something guaranteed to make an editor cringe and place your story on the rejection pile.

How do I set my story out?

In the chapter on article writing, I explained how you sometimes need to send out a query letter/email to see if the editor would be interested in your idea before sending the full article. In the case of the short story, there's no need to do this – you just send your complete story. If you're not sure if the magazine takes unsolicited fiction scripts, you can email them or give them a quick call just to check.

Setting out a short story is very similar to setting out an article – take a look back at the page on writing articles for a reminder. If you're sending your short story by post (like a few article markets, some short story publications still prefer stories to be sent to them this way), you'll need a cover sheet and a covering letter. If it's by email, you won't need the cover sheet, but do remember to include all your contact details in your covering email. In your covering letter/email there's no need to detail what your story is about, unless they ask you to in their guidelines. Otherwise, you just need a short introduction, including the title of your story and the word count. The main body should detail a little bit about your writing and how you think readers of the magazine will enjoy your story. Bring the letter to a close by thanking them for their time and stating that you look forward to hearing from them shortly.

Now try this

It's so tempting to start with a story for one of the women's weeklies. You may be fortunate enough to have a story accepted straight away. I've known writers who have been in that exact position, only for them to find it difficult to gain publication for their next stories. As I've suggested, you can start small, with the small press market, or you can try writing for a variety of publications. Just make sure you always study the publication you're going to write for carefully to make sure you're along the right lines when you write your own story.

Stuck for ideas on what to write about? You'll find plenty of ideas for short stories in the next chapter.

For examples of published stories, see page 126.

Sizzling Story Ideas

After reading numerous short stories in your research for short story markets, you should feel inspired, with a plethora of story ideas of your own whizzing round in your mind. Maybe you have, or you just have a couple of tentative ideas. On the other hand, you might have had several, but you've already used them and new ideas aren't coming. Here are a few suggestions to get those creative juices flowing:

Story title

Thinking up a title for a story can often ignite an idea. For example, 'A New Beginning'. This title promotes an image of someone starting afresh. Perhaps a wife who has been the victim of domestic violence for a number of years takes that brave step and leaves her husband. How does she do it? Does he come after her? What does her new beginning involve? See how the story is already starting to develop in your mind. The same title could take you in a completely different direction. The new beginning could relate to a refugee who's fleeing oppression and starting life in a new country. Or your story could be about a town that's recovering after a tragic chain of events. A title can conjure up all sorts of possibilities for an exciting and gripping story.

Writing exercise

Here are some other ideas to try. Take each one in turn and jot down ideas that come to mind.

The Dark Place

The Rendezvous

Flashback

Watching

The Unborn

People watching

Walk down the road and you might encounter a man walking a dog, an old lady, the postman and so on. You may not take much notice of them, but is there something about them to trigger an idea for a story? Was the man with the dog looking a little nervous? In real life, he may have a work assignment he's worried about. In your story he could be thinking about declaring his undying love for a work colleague. Is his love returned? Or maybe he encounters another dog walker every day – a woman who's fallen in love with him, yet he barely notices her. Here, you've got an idea for a romance story with several possible endings.

Let's take the old lady. She may be a lovely lady who you know very well, though in your story the old lady has a dark secret. Does she have lots of visitors who never seem to come out of her house? The idea of a horror story comes to mind. Or, for a crime story, the character of the old lady could be a drug dealer who's been on the run for many years. Has she turned over a new leaf or is she up to no good?

Writing exercise

Here are a few ideas for characters and situations you could make a story out of. What immediately comes to mind once you've read each one? Write your ideas down:

A young boy on his own.

Is he lost? Has he run away? Maybe he's about to be snatched by an opportunist passing by in a car. Or he's an alien with an agenda.

_____

_____

_____

_____

_____

_____

_____

_____

_____

_____

_____

_____

_____

_____

_____

_____

_____

_____

A homeless woman sitting on an old sleeping bag, seemingly lost in her own world.

What's her story? Has she lost everything after being conned by someone? She might have been thrown out of the family home by her parents because of her unruly behaviour. Or is she an undercover policewoman watching a house opposite?

_____

_____

_____

_____

_____

_____

_____

_____

_____

_____

_____

_____

_____

_____

_____

A mother with a child in a pushchair.

Does she have a smile on her face? Has she just found out she's pregnant again – with twins? Or is she thinking about the man she's meeting that night – in secret? Instead of a smile, she's crying. She could have postnatal depression and feel as if her life is spiralling out of control.

A group of school children racing past, shouting and jeering.

Have they just bullied another child and left them in tears or worse? Or are they celebrating something special, like getting exam results or the end of school? Is one hanging back? Perhaps they didn't do so well in their exams and don't want to go home to tell their parents, or maybe they're being taken out of school as their parents are moving abroad and they'll be leaving all their friends and everything they know behind them.

_____

_____

_____

_____

_____

_____

_____

_____

_____

_____

_____

_____

_____

A man running down the road.

Is he running to catch a train? What will happen if he misses it? He could dash out into the road and be hit by a car, or he might be the one to knock someone else over. Or is he late for a meeting with someone? Who is he meeting? Perhaps he's running from a zombie and the world is about to change beyond all recognition.

_____

_____

_____

_____

_____

_____

_____

_____

_____

_____

_____

_____

_____

_____

Location

A tranquil beach with a blazing riot of a sunset and the gentle lapping of waves into shore is the perfect setting for a romance story, but more mundane locations can also generate a compelling story idea. How about your local market? You may be poking and prodding at the apples when you see a child out of the corner of your eye. In your story, the child could steal an apple from the stall. Perhaps the child has run away from a terrible homelife or maybe he/she is doing it as a dare to look good in front of a group of friends. Another possibility is a bully, lurking in wait, ready to taunt the child if he/she doesn't carry out the act. One option is to tell the story through the child's eyes. This always stands out and adds an extra element of emotion. So, as well as thinking up locations for your stories, take note of what's around you. Inspiration often strikes where and when you least expect it.

Writing exercise

Want some more? The following are just a few locations to stimulate places for an entertaining and compelling story. The story threads suggested here may bring others to mind. Write down your ideas:

An old house that's been boarded up for a long time.

Walking past one evening, your character notices there's a light on. Who is in there? A ghost? A squatter? An axe-murderer? A group of teenagers?

_____

_____

_____

_____

_____

_____

_____

_____

_____

_____

_____

_____

_____

_____

_____

A supermarket. A woman starts screaming.

What's wrong with her? What/who has she seen? Or is she mentally ill? There's a crash from outside. What's going on? An accident? An attack?

A bedroom.

Has someone died in the bedroom? Now? Or years before? Perhaps the bedroom has a secret door into another world, or it's just a hiding place for secrets.

_____

_____

_____

_____

_____

_____

_____

_____

_____

_____

_____

_____

_____

_____

_____

Some woods.

A person may be killed, or become lost in the woods. Or maybe something happened there years before - something supernatural and unexplained. It could be happening all over again. Alternatively, two dog walkers meet in the woods and love blossoms.

A school reunion.

Could feuds have festered over the years? Will first loves be there and once more rekindled? Is there someone there who shouldn't be?

_____

_____

_____

_____

_____

_____

_____

_____

_____

_____

_____

_____

_____

_____

_____

_____

_____

_____

Books and DVDs

Bookshelves and/or DVD racks are commonly found in our houses, featuring all manner of titles. For example, *The Grudge*, *When Will There Be Good News?* and *Robin Hood*. Think about each title in turn and you should find all sorts of ideas for short stories start to come to mind.

Let's take *The Grudge* to start with. This is a well-known horror movie, but your story doesn't have to be in the horror genre. You could write a romance – about a long-term grudge held between two neighbours. How they resolve it and get together is up to you. Or perhaps the title starts you thinking about a crime story where a grudge gets out of hand.

When Will There Be Good News? is a book by best-selling author Kate Atkinson featuring the loveable but always in trouble, private investigator, Jackson Brodie. But the good news or lack of it doesn't have to relate to a crime story. What 'news' ideas come to mind? Happy news – an engagement, passing an exam, getting the all-clear from the doctor, a missing child found…any of these can be turned into stories. What about bad news? The possibilities are endless and will make for an equally compelling story.

Most of us are familiar with the story of Robin Hood. What about a Robin Hood story with a twist? Maybe it's the Sheriff of Nottingham who's the good guy or why can't Robin be a woman? Re-writing well-known, classic stories can make for very entertaining reads. They're always popular in small press magazines.

Writing exercise

None coming to mind? Here are some for you:

It Happened One Night

Unforgiven

The Last Amen

The Keeper of Lost Things

Crash

An opening line

It can be fun to give yourself a first line to work on. For example, 'If only he hadn't opened the newspaper at page 9...' What happens next? Is there something hidden in the paper? A secret message? Or maybe the gentleman in question sees a photo of himself on page 9, somewhere he knows he's never been and with someone he's never met. This particular story thread could be turned into a crime story, a sci-fi story about cloning, a humorous story about mistaken identity and so on.

Here's another first line: 'She peered through the darkness...' Is there something lurking in the darkness ready to grab her? A vampire? A zombie? There might not be anything in the darkness; the woman may have heard a sound outside and gone to investigate, but when she returns to the house, she finds that's where the danger is lurking.

Writing exercise

I'm sure you can come up with plenty of intriguing opening lines of your own. Here are some more to set you thinking:

- I knew she was dead even though the dull eyes stared back at me, mocking me, tempting me to raise the knife once more.

- "I didn't mean to do it. I'm not bad," she said, her pale blue eyes awash with tears.

- Just one more, that's all I was going to take.

- "How are things?" he asked, "I know it's been hard for you."

- I can't remember my mummy and daddy.

PUBLICATION GUARANTEED (Well, almost!)

A last line

Similarly, a last line can trigger ideas for a story. For example, 'Yes, it was definitely time for a change'. A change of what? What has led your character to think things need to change? Has he/she gone through a traumatic time at work and wants a change of career? Your main protagonist could have been in a disastrous relationship and feels now is the time to make a stand. Their parents may have been oppressive and your lead character has stood up to them by the end of your story.

Another last line for you is, 'He knew life was never going to be the same again'. Why not? Has your character been the victim of a crime that's left him scarred, but he's determined he'll get through it? Has he survived a zombie apocalypse and lost everyone he knows? He may have come through a quest in a fantasy story and he can't return to his world. There are all sorts of possibilities.

Writing exercise

Here are a few more last lines for you:

- All he could do was whisper, "I'm sorry, I'm sorry."

- Somehow, I think I'm going to like it here.

- They walked on, leaving the grey and gloomy buildings behind them, neither one looking back.

- Her mouth gaped open; she was sure it hadn't been there before.

- She took a deep breath, stepped forward and took his hand.

And a few more

Other ideas include looking at a fairy tale in a different light. What would happen if the well-renowned shoe actually fitted one of the ugly sisters? This puts a completely new slant on things. Magazines and the TV are another source of story ideas. They're full of different characters and situations, which can create an idea for a story if you look at them from a different angle.

COMPETITIONS

Is it a dream of yours to win a writing competition? To have your writing truly recognised? To know your story was the best? As a winner of several writing competitions, I know first-hand how special writing competitions are. Doing well in a competition changes how you think about your writing. It gives it authority, whether you're shortlisted or a winner. It's something to put at the top of your writing CV and it can lead to other work. Succeeding in competitions made me realise I *could* write and if my writing was good enough to win such well-known competitions, it was good enough to send out to editors.

Another attraction of writing competitions is they're great fun to enter. Many competitions have cash prizes and publish the winning entries in print form, in a magazine or anthology, while others publish on the Internet. Some organisers also provide a critique to the entrant in exchange for just a few pounds. This can be invaluable as all too often editors reject our writing with no hint of why our precious piece of work isn't suitable.

How do I find out about writing competitions?

You'll find numerous writing competitions just by typing 'writing competitions' into your search engine. The writing resources I've covered earlier, such as *Writing Magazine*, list lots of competitions and hold regular ones of their own.

Top Tip

Writing competitions have closing dates. It's so easy to miss the deadline — especially if you're entering by post. So do make sure you send your story in well before the deadline. If it's a day late, it won't be accepted.

So how do I write a winning story?

We all differ in the type of short story we enjoy — and so it stands to reason a story one judge might enjoy, another may not. I once entered a writing competition and had my story slated in the accompanying critique. But I had faith in my story and entered it into another competition. It won. So it just goes to show.

Having said that, it's good to get a feel for what makes a winning story and so it can be useful to analyse prize winning stories. Take a look back at the chapter on short stories and how to analyse them. When you're looking at the winning stories from a competition, think about what made them stand out. Did the writing flow from one image to the other? Did the story urge you to read on to the very end? Was it character-driven or plot-driven? Some competition organisers write reports on the winning entries, highlighting exactly what the judge was looking for and why the winners ticked all the right boxes. When they do, read them. This can be very helpful for moving forward in your competition writing.

Here are a few pointers to help you make your story stand out in a competition:

- **Think outside the box.** The same old storyline is something that gets a judge's back up straight away. An example of such a story is where the downtrodden wife appears to have no idea of her husband's infidelities, but it turns out she knows just what's going on, kills her husband and gets away with it. Another story that will put a judge off is one where a woman is taking a walk with her dog through the woods and comes across a cottage she's never noticed before. An old lady invites her in for a cup of tea. The next day the woman takes some biscuits as a thank you to the lady but discovers the cottage is dilapidated and the old lady died years ago.

- **So how do you make your story original?** Think outside the box. For a ghost story, the ghost could be a famous person. Who would he/she choose to haunt and why? This has enormous scope for a humorous and entertaining story, which will make a judge laugh out loud.

- **Or perhaps the ghost is that of a soldier killed while serving in Iraq.** Does he go to see his family and find them unable to cope with his death? This would make a touching story, adding an element of emotion and forcing a judge to feel moved.

- **You might want to write a story about witches.** It's easy to conjure up an image of a woman with black hair, a long black cloak, black cat and broomstick. But can you think of others who aren't labelled witches but behave very much like them? What about a group of girls at secondary school who bully another vulnerable girl? This would certainly make a compelling story.

- **A story about a siege, which takes place in a library,** is surely something a judge wouldn't expect. What events led up to it? Who's involved? There are lots of possibilities to make an unusual and exciting story.

- **Unusual viewpoint.** A story told from a different viewpoint can often catch the eye. However, stories where the writer attempts the twist-in-the-tale of the narrator turning out to be a cat or dog have been seen by a judge many times over. Nonetheless, a story featuring someone who we wouldn't normally expect to be a narrator will stand out.

- **Stories seen through the eyes of a child** can be particularly effective. How about a little boy in a children's home rocking himself to sleep, never believing anyone will want to adopt him? This tugs at the heart-strings straight away. Another narrator could be a young teenager battling to cope with his parents' divorce.

- **A character we wouldn't usually associate with being a narrator** is the fairy on top of the Christmas tree. What goings-on between the family members does she witness?

- **A story narrated by a celebrity makeup artist** who hears all sorts of secrets, but who is treated as if she isn't there, has all the makings of an explosive story.

- **Humour.** A judge often has hundreds of entries to read through. A significant number will be full of misery and woe, so a story that makes a judge break out into a smile comes as a welcome relief. It's likely the story will be put to one side to be looked at again. Though the humour mustn't be forced or the script full of exclamation marks; these act like a neon sign to ensure the judge knows exactly which parts are supposed to be side-splittingly funny.

- **A modern take on a fairy tale can make a great humorous story**. For example, a bungling burglar as a modern 'Goldie' in Goldilocks and the three bears. Returning to the topic of unusual viewpoints, an amusing story could feature the donkey that carried Mary to Bethlehem as narrator.

- **Adhere to the rules.** Read through any competition rules carefully. For example, there's likely to be a word limit. Even if your word count is one word over the limit, your entry will be disqualified. If all the other entrants have kept within the word limit, why should you be allowed extra? The amount of entries instantly disqualified simply because the entrant hasn't stuck to the rules is surprising.

Top Tip

Don't just enter one competition and wait for the result. You might not hear back for a few weeks or even months. Once you have submitted one, start on another story for another competition so you always have something in the pipeline.

Fees

Many writing competitions have a set fee. They can seem expensive – upwards of £8 per entry so it can get expensive if you keep entering competitions. But there are some with a smaller entry fee and there are free competitions. Those asking for a high entry fee often offer very good prize money, say £500, or even £1000. They're also often the most widely known ones, so there's a lot of prestige associated with winning one of them and they'll likely attract lots of entries. You'll be up against stiff competition, so your story must be spot on in every way – in terms of the story as well as ensuring there aren't any mistakes.

Top Tip

Most short story competitions specify stories entered must be unpublished and not entered into any other competitions. This is a must. If it's discovered your entry has appeared in an issue of last year's local paper, in an old short story magazine, or has won another competition, your entry will be disqualified immediately.

How do I set my story out?

We've covered how to set a short story out and how to send it to an editor, but with a competition, it's a little different. For a start, your name shouldn't appear anywhere on the story itself. This is to ensure you can't be identified by the judge. If you're posting your entry, there may be an entry form and you may also need to send a cover sheet with all your contact details on (like the example cover sheet given earlier). If you're sending it online, some competitions require you to send your story via an email, as an attachment, so you can include all your contact details in the body of the covering email. Others have a facility where you fill in an entry form online, with all your details and then you upload your story and send it through their website. It'll be made clear in the rules or competition pages.

Some competitions prefer stories to be sent in double spacing and a particular font. Again, this will be covered in the rules, or competition pages, if they want it a certain way.

Top Tip

If you don't come anywhere, keep writing and entering competitions. Sometimes it can take a while before you start to make the shortlist. Keep going – next time you might be amongst the winners. You only need one chance.

Now try this

In the examples I've given you, the short stories were a variety of lengths. One of them was a 100-word story. Have a go at writing one of that length. There still needs to be a beginning, middle and end. Stories of that length also often have a twist. It's a fun way to start, helps you keep your writing nice and tight, and you can build from there.

For examples of prize-winning stories, see page 139.

Examples of Published Work

The following are examples of published readers' letters, fillers, articles and short stories, together with some prize-winning competition entries, to give you an idea of what editors and judges are looking for. From the information you've read throughout the book on how to analyse your market, as well as all the tips and insights, see if you can work out why these were accepted/won prizes.

Readers' Letters:

Letter to one of the women's weeklies, sent with a photo:

I found this photo of my nan and grandad, taken over fifty years ago at my auntie and uncle's wedding. They were wonderful grandparents and don't they make a handsome couple?!

Letter to a general interest publication about an article published in a previous publication:

Your 'Outdoor Cinema' article brought back happy memories from a year ago when my partner and I sat in the grounds of Wollaton Hall, Nottingham. It was there Batman, The Dark Knight Rises, was filmed and we were there to watch a special screening. I'll always remember the screen bursting into life and Christian Bale appearing, with the menacing and eerie hall to my back, creating an extraordinary sense of atmosphere.

I wasn't aware other places held outdoor screenings. I'll certainly be looking for some more.

Letter to a health magazine about the topic of complementary therapies:

Even in this modern day and age, where complementary medicine is becoming more widely accepted, there are still people, including doctors, who are sceptical of its benefits. Acupuncture and homeopathy have been used on animals with brilliant results. If that isn't proof, then what is?

Letter to a TV magazine about a programme recently aired at the time:

'Fool Britannia' was like a breath of fresh air. All too often we're presented with comedy shows where the humour is forced. Not so with Dom Joly's new show. I spent the whole half hour laughing out loud. There was only one problem - half an hour wasn't long enough!

Letter to a women's weekly about a funny anecdote. Sent in time for Halloween:

Last Halloween, Mum and I were going out for the evening so Dad was left in charge of giving out sweets to any trick or treaters.

When we came back, Dad seemed to have accumulated more sweets than ever! "I like this trick or treat lark," he said, with a big smile, "when I opened the door, the children asked me if I wanted a trick or treat. Of course I wanted a treat, so I took a sweet from them. That's really kind of them, isn't it? Though, they did look a bit surprised."

Mum and I couldn't believe it! I hope Dad gets it right for this Halloween otherwise there might be some very upset children!

Letter to a national newspaper about a report they recently featured:

Well, I certainly didn't expect to see Afghan children skateboarding in the centre pages of last week's paper, but I'm so glad I did. The children have suffered so much and many of them have only known a life of heartache and pain, so it was wonderful to see happy faces having fun. A truly uplifting report.

Fillers:

Filler for a general interest publication inviting funny true-life anecdotes:

Mum sent Dad to the shops to buy some pork chops. Dad couldn't find them so he thought it best to ask an assistant.

"Do you have any loin cloths?" he asked.

"Sorry, Tarzan, we don't have any so you won't be swinging through the trees tonight," she quipped.

Dad then realised he may not have asked for loin chops as he'd thought…

Filler for a national newspaper for their music slot:

When I was growing up in the 1970s, Smurfs were the latest craze and like any young child, I was mad about them. Some of my friends had lots of them, but times were hard for Mum and Dad and so they couldn't afford to buy me all the newest toys. I was a little envious of my friends, but they'd often 'loan' me the odd Smurf or two so we could all play together.

Then Dad came home one day with a record. He had a big grin on his face as he gave it to me. I remember looking at him a little blankly. He had lots of records he'd often listen to – from The Shadows, to The Everly Brothers, to Val Doonican. I wasn't particularly keen on any of them so I wasn't sure why he'd bought me a record – until he played it. The Smurf song is terrible, utterly terrible, but extremely catchy (even now!) and as a young six-year-old, I adored it.

And what's more, none of my friends had a copy. For once I had something they didn't! But, as they did with me, I shared and we'd often happily be found singing the odd, 'La, la, la, la, la, la, la, la, la, la' - they really did seem to go on forever.

I was even lucky enough to be given three of my own Smurfs – one male and one female and then the most wondrous of Smurfs – The Astronaut Space Smurf. It felt like ten Christmases rolled into one when Dad gave me the plastic helmeted Smurf. He was even better than the record (don't tell Dad) and I took him everywhere. Alas, one of the neighbours' boys got hold of him and threw him across the garden. I will never forget the day when I picked the Smurf's broken body (well, his helmet was cracked) and carried him inside, tears streaming down my cheeks.

It wasn't long after that I grew out of the Smurfs and moved on to the next craze. Though, they've made the odd comeback over recent years and I must admit I always have a smile to myself when I see them. I've heard Britney Spears recorded a song for one of the Smurfs' films. Sorry, Britney, but you're no Father Abraham.

Filler for a women's weekly inviting funny true-life anecdotes about men:

One Sunday morning, Mum and I heard screams coming from the bathroom. We rushed in, expecting the worst and stared at Dad.

"I'm coughing up blood!" he shrieked in panic.

Mum looked into his mouth and shook her head in disbelief and told him: "You've brushed your teeth too hard, you fool!"

Filler for a general interest publication inviting short travel experiences:

For two years a friend of mine had been urging me to visit her in Dubai, where she was working as a teacher. But I have to admit I really wasn't keen. Perhaps I'd read too many negative newspaper reports about rules and regulations. Or maybe I simply thought it too modern and ugly. I was to be proved very wrong.

Eventually I gave in to the pleas and travelled to Dubai to stay with my friend for five days. At the airport, I was given a warm welcome and instantly I knew I was going to love my time in Dubai.

It really is a place of wonder and opulence, with dazzling delights at every turn. I thought I'd been to a big shopping mall before but never have I been to one with an underwater zoo, ice rink, dinosaur, fountain with diving men (well, not real ones, but it's a sight to behold all the same), flight simulator, or the entrance to the world's tallest building. Oh, and that's without even beginning to mention the plethora of shops — some full of the latest fashions, others dripping with sparkling jewellery, while the senses are assailed with a riot of sounds and scents.

As for the world's tallest building, The Burj Khalifa, when I stepped out of the elevator and took a first peek out the window, on level 148, all I could think was wow, wow, wow! Huge hotels and towering skyscrapers looked miniscule. I felt as if I was looking down at a model village. Yet, I'd stood near some of those buildings and marvelled at their structure and presence. As I walked onto an outside viewing platform, the wind whipping around me, the stifling scorch of the heat assaulting me, looking over the Dubai vista, I felt as if I'd been taken to a whole new world. It's a moment I'll never forget.

But I didn't just remain at The Dubai Mall during my stay. There were certainly plenty of other sights to enjoy. My friend took me to the soft golden sands of Jumeirah Beach, to a lavish brunch, brimming with tasty treats, as well as to a traditional and vibrant Arabian market (a souk).

There were also other trips planned — to Atlantis Aquaventure Waterpark and to a mosque, but there's only so much you can pack into five days. It looks like I may well have to go back…

Filler for a women's weekly asking for photos and captions of readers' cute kids:

My daughter insists she wears the trousers — even if they are her mum's!

A photo of the child in question, aged three at the time, wearing the writer's baggy jogging bottoms and them engulfing her, accompanied the filler.

Filler to a women's weekly asking a beauty question for their beauty pages:

How do I apply blusher correctly? I either find I look too pale where I haven't put enough on, or I overdo it and end up looking bright red in the face!

Articles:

An article for a national newspaper about a special family member:

My Grandad – Master of Coppit and Boxes

Just before my grandad died, he said to me, "Don't ever grow up. I never have."

He was ninety-three years old and I was thirty-six.

Everyone thinks their grandad is special and mine certainly was. Father to six and grandfather to ten, he had such a way with children, always coming up with fun ideas and ways to make us all laugh.

What I remember most about Grandad are the games. I was only seven years old when my other grandad had a stroke and had to be taken to hospital. Mum didn't drive and the hospital was in a town a good few miles away. Grandad gave her a lift there several times so she could see her dad. I always tagged along and while Mum went to see her father, Grandad would sit with me and play games. My favourite was 'Boxes'. I'm sure it has a 'proper' name, but we called it 'The Boxes Game'.

It was very simple: you drew several rows of dots across a piece of paper. Then you took turns to draw a line, from one dot to another. The idea was not to let your opponent make a box. If you did, then your opponent would claim the box and insert their initial. Once you made one box, it often had a domino effect and led to you being able to claim one box after another. I always won, but I'm pretty sure Grandad let me.

Another game we played, though this time at his house, was 'Coppit'. It was a board game and similar in nature to Ludo, though oh so much better. Instead of counters, each player had a coloured cone/hat shaped playing piece. You started off on your home 'base'. The object was to move out of your base, then to capture, or 'cop', your opponents' pieces by landing on top of them, shouting out, "Coppit" and then carrying them back to your base, and 'imprisoning' them there. Now, Coppit was a game Grandad didn't ever let me win. Much to my very miffed younger self's annoyance.

In this particular photo (sent with the article and appearing in the paper), *Grandad was working at one of the local garages on reception. Always a man to keep busy, he took on the job when he retired from his main work. He'd always loved cars and relished working at the garage. One of the employees still speaks fondly of him, though he said one day Grandad wanted to strip a car down and then put it back together again. "He was fine taking it apart, but the problem came when he had to remember where all the parts went. It didn't quite look like a car when he'd finished with it so he had to have a bit of help."*

He may not have been a master of cars, but he was certainly a master of Coppit and Boxes — and a master grandad.

An article for a nostalgia magazine about a childhood memory:

Bunty is the Best

"You can't have Bunty. I have Bunty. You can have Mandy."

My friend's words chilled me. It was 1979 and we were both seven years old. At that grand old age, I had grown out of Twinkle comic and was ready to move on.

I'd stood for ages at the newsagent's, with Mum tutting beside me, as my eyes lit up at the array of comics on display — The Dandy, The Beano, Mandy, Bunty, Judy, Jackie (a bit too old for me at the time) and several others. Mum didn't understand. To have a weekly comic was a wonderful treat. When Dad first bought me Twinkle when I was five, I'd fallen in love with it. The pages were bursting with colour, the stories (absolutely dire, of course, but brilliant to a young girl) dazzling and entertaining and then there was the cut-out doll, with cut-out clothes to dress her in. And her choice of wardrobe was mine, all mine. Well, all two outfits, that is. But I loved her and I loved cut-out dolls.

So when the stories in Twinkle became too twee and 'beneath me', it was time to take the next step in comics for girls.

The Dandy and The Beano looked fun but more for boys. Mandy and Judy looked quite good, but when I saw Bunty had a cut-out doll every week, that was it. There was no contest — until I told my friend.

She was adamant. Bunty was hers and I wasn't allowed to have it as well. I was so upset. I didn't want Mandy, I wanted Bunty. I can't quite remember how it was resolved. Perhaps our mothers sorted it out or maybe we sorted it out for ourselves as I started to take Bunty each week and my friend decided she preferred Mandy after all!

I couldn't wait to get my hands on the comic every week. Woe betide the paper boy if he brought it late. I would then settle down and read it from cover to cover. Thinking back to the story strips makes me wonder who on Earth came up with the titles. Clearly someone who liked her alliteration. There was Catch the Cat, Tina of Tumbledown Towers, Sandra's Sad Secret, Lessons from Lindy, In Petra's Place, Donna's Double Life and many more.

My favourite story was The Four Marys. It's arguably the most popular and well-known one, running from when the comic was first launched in 1958 to its end in 2001. Reminiscent of Enid Blyton's St. Clare's and Malory Towers books, which centred around girls at boarding school, The Four Mary's featured stories about four girls at St. Elmo's Boarding School for Girls. I loved the scrapes the girls found themselves in, but no matter what happened, it all ended well.

Once I'd devoured the stories, I then turned to the back page and to Bunty's Cut-Out Wardrobe. I don't know what it was about the cut-out dolls I loved so much. I'd always loved playing with dolls' houses and figures and making up stories. I had a Sindy doll, but she only had a couple of outfits so perhaps that was it. Here was this young girl, albeit a paper one, with a different wardrobe every week. Money was tight in the 70s and I didn't often have new clothes myself so that may also have been part of the appeal. Additionally, I was fascinated by the tabs on the clothes, which you had to fold around the doll (just squares of paper, but to me they were ingenious).

Then there were the Christmas annuals. I always put the Bunty annual on my Christmas lists and over the years was lucky enough to find the 1980, 1981 and 1982 editions in my stocking.

Secondary school followed. At eleven, Bunty and cut-out dolls were still very much part of my life. But I soon found out they weren't part of the other girls' lives; it just wasn't considered acceptable or cool to like either.

So my love affair with Bunty and cut-out dolls was over. I didn't throw the comics and annuals away. I wasn't ready to part with them just yet. Each comic and annual was placed lovingly in a pile in the bottom of my wardrobe and taken out for a sneaky read now and then.

My weekly magazine (note the word change from the now considered babyish 'comic') became Jackie, then I 'progressed' to Smash Hits before Just Seventeen caught my eye. But none of them measured up to Bunty.

I don't know what happened to those comics and annuals in the bottom of my wardrobe. I don't remember ever getting rid of them. But they must have gone at some stage.

My mum couldn't wait to give me one of my Christmas presents this year – a 1978 Bunty annual she'd managed to get hold of. She asked if I remembered it as she was sure it was around the time I'd first started to get Bunty. I didn't like to tell her I hadn't yet discovered the delights of Bunty then. But it didn't matter. I loved every page of it. Not only did it feature an extra length The Four Marys story, there was also a cut-out doll. But it was no ordinary cut-out doll, it was a special Cut-out and Colour Wardrobe cut-out doll. Heaven.

An article to a cat magazine about unusual folktales about cats:

Cat Tales of the Unexpected

There have been all sorts of fascinating folktales about cats passed down over the years. Many of them are well-known and you'll have heard them time and time again, from stories of witches' cats, to how tabby cats came to have the 'M' on their forehead, to fables about cats and dogs. So it's always good to come across some news ones – and ones that'll leave you smiling, which hopefully these entertaining tales will.

Why do cats eat first and wash afterwards?

Right from when we're small, we're always told to wash our hands before we eat. So why do cats do it the other way round? Our first tale will enlighten you:

One day, a cat caught a mouse and was just about to eat it for her supper.

The mouse cried, "Where are your manners?! You should wash your face and paws before you eat."

The cat felt ashamed of herself and so she quickly licked her paws and washed her face.

The mouse, of course, saw this as an ideal opportunity to run away!

The cat learned from this and ever since then, they always eat first and wash themselves after.

I'll just help myself

This Jewish tale highlights what we all already know – when it comes to food, a cat isn't daft!

When the world was first created, God called every newly made creature together and asked them all where they wanted to get their food from. God turned to the cat and asked her, "Would you like your food to come from the farmer, the fisherman or the shopkeeper?"

The cat thought about this for a moment and shook her head. "Please don't go to any trouble on my behalf. All I ask is the housewife leaves the kitchen door open and then I'll help myself."

And doesn't that sound just like a cat?!

The snake in the grass

Our next story is one of American Indian origin, where the cat saves the day. Of course she does!

Many, many years ago, in the days animals could talk and spirits lived in the forest, a baby boy was born and with one look, his mother knew he was descended from the gods. He was known as a gentle, caring boy and when he became an adult, he was known as the Magician.

A great plague came and swept through the village where the Magician lived. Luckily, he knew the antidote – the silver-leafed plant and so he headed into the forest to find it so he could save his people.

In the forest lurked Irmah, the serpent. Anyone who had encountered Irmah never returned. But the Magician was unafraid. His dog wanted to go with his master, but the Magician said no as it was too dangerous. But the Magician's cat, who had been listening, secretly followed him.

When the Magician was deep in the forest, the little cat leapt onto his shoulder and told her master how much she loved him. "When everyone shunned me, you didn't. You showed me kindness. So I will be your protector and save you from the serpent."

The Magician smiled and thanked the cat, but he knew a tiny cat would be no match for the mighty and fearsome serpent.

That night, the serpent snaked its way closer and closer to the sleeping Magician. But the little cat had been waiting and pounced on Irmah. Soon the pair were engaged in a terrifying tussle, but the little cat didn't give up and emerged the victor at sunrise.

The Magician was amazed and cried, "However can I repay you, little cat?"

And what did the little cat want in return? "I'd like to no longer be treated as an outcast. May I now be allowed to enter the wigwams and be everyone's friend?"

The Magician instantly agreed so the cat was no longer an outcast.

The pub cat and the pub mouse

During my research into cats and their lives, I've come across a pub cat or two, but I have to admit never a pub mouse! Well, here's a delightful Irish tale about both.

One night, when the pub was closed and all the customers had gone home, the pub cat was chasing the pub mouse. It's said it was one of the greatest cat and mouse chases ever! The pair dashed across the floor, over the bar and till, clanging bottles on shelves and weaving between stools, nearly knocking them over.

Big trouble was in store – the pub landlord had been busy that day and had left the soap out in an unexpected place. The mouse was running so fast he skidded on it and splash! Before he knew it, he was paddling away in a barrel of beer. The poor mouse couldn't swim and saw his life flash before his very eyes.

The cat casually peered over the top of the barrel.

"Help! Save me, save me! Please," begged the mouse, swallowing a mouthful of beer.

The cat grinned from ear to ear and licked his lips.

"I don't care if you eat me," cried the mouse, "just get me out of here. I don't want to drown in a barrel of beer!"

The cat agreed and scooped the mouse out with his paw. He placed the mouse on a tea towel beside some washed up glasses.

But the mouse was no fool and quick as a flash, he was off.

The cat was furious. "You gave me your word I could eat you if I saved you from drowning in a barrel of beer."

The mouse glanced back at the cat. "Didn't your mother warn you not to believe what someone who's been drinking says?"

And he turned tail and ran!

How to name your cat

When you chose your cat's name, I'm sure you thought about it very carefully, perhaps thinking about cats in books, or films, or you may have had a name in mind as soon as you saw your cat.

In the following Chinese story, Mr Chi-Yen had a cat he held in such high esteem he called it 'Tiger'. His neighbour was very unimpressed and told him, "The tiger is a ferocious animal, but it isn't as mysterious as a dragon and cats are very mysterious. You should change your cat's name to 'Dragon'."

Another neighbour advised Mr Chi-Yen that dragons flew up into the clouds and rested on them so clouds were better than dragons so he should change his cat's name to 'Cloud'.

Well, some of Mr Chi-Yen's other neighbours weren't having that and one said, "The wind scatters the dark clouds when they scuttle across the sky. So the wind is more powerful than the clouds. And cats are powerful. You should change your cat's name to 'Wind'.

The neighbours began talking over one another, with one suggesting that when the wind whips up into a thunderstorm, we shelter within our four walls. So the cat should be called 'Wall'. Another shouted out that 'Rat' should be the name of Mr Chi-Yen's cat, as rats can chew through walls.

Mr Ch-Yen had heard enough and had the last word, "And that is why he will be called 'Cat'."

I hope you've enjoyed these entertaining tales. And, where cats are concerned, there's sure to be many more!

Short Stories:

A short story written for one of the women's weeklies:

Meant To Be

"Lizzie Waldron, is that really you?" Tess cried.

"Tess Baker! It must have been at least twenty years since I've seen you," Lizzie said, with a huge smile on her face.

Katie pulled at her mother's trouser leg, wrinkling her nose as this Tess woman hugged and kissed her mother. Katie pulled at the material again. Nothing. Just more hugs and kisses. Now her mother was crying.

"You look wonderful, Tess," Lizzie said, looking Tess up and down.

Katie shook her head. No, she didn't. She had a white T-shirt on with splodges all down the front and her skirt was all wrinkled. Her hair was sticking up, too. Her mother would never let Katie go out dressed like that.

"You, too, Lizzie. You've not aged a bit," Tess replied, laughing.

Katie looked at her mother. That wasn't right. Her mother was old. All grown-ups were old.

"Isn't this wonderful?" Lizzie said.

Katie pouted. That word again. Wonderful. It definitely was not wonderful. This was supposed to be her special day. It was her first day at pre-school and her mother seemed to have forgotten all about it.

"We were inseparable, weren't we? We said we'd always be best friends," Tess sighed. "We were until Mum and Dad decided to move and I went to a different school. We vowed to stay in touch, but we never did."

"And here we are, twenty odd years later, with our own children. It's Katie's first day today," Lizzie said, pushing Katie forward.

"My Ben's been coming here for six months," Tess said, patting a small boy's head.

126

Katie stared at the boy. She hadn't noticed him before. She wished she hadn't now. He was poking his tongue out at her. How rude. She poked hers right back.

"Katie! You know not to do that. I'm so sorry, Ben," Lizzie said.

"Don't worry. They'll be best of friends in no time. Just like we were. They'll probably end up getting married," Tess chuckled.

"Wouldn't that be wonderful?" Lizzie grinned.

Katie scowled. She hated boys. They smelt and were made of worms. She was never going to get married and especially not to Ben Baker.

"Look at them both. Katie Waldron and Ben Baker. It's meant to be," Lizzie said, firmly.

...

Katie soon settled down at pre-school. She loved everything about it - the painting, gluing, story-time - everything - apart from Ben Baker.

"He pulled my hair!" Katie yelled.

"Didn't! She pushed me," Ben screamed.

"Not again, you two," the pre-school teacher said, frowning, "let's see if we can try and get on a little bit better, shall we?"

"No," said Katie, stamping her foot.

"No," said Ben, folding his arms across his chest.

"Mrs Waldron, Mrs Baker, I'm afraid things haven't improved between Katie and Ben," the pre-school teacher told them at pick-up time.

"They will. They're going to get married one day," Tess smiled.

"Katie Waldron and Ben Baker. It's meant to be," Lizzie said, firmly.

...

"It's really not meant to be," Lizzie said, sadly. "I can't believe you're going."

Tess blinked back the tears. "I know. It's Daniel's job. The transfer came out of the blue. But the money's good, so he's got to take it."

"It's just I've loved renewing our friendship. It's like those twenty years have never been. I'm going to miss you so much, Tess."

"Me, too. And those children. They may dislike each other now, but their friendship would have come, then romance and love."

"I know. Katie Waldron and Ben Baker. It was meant to be," Lizzie agreed.

"Still, we're only moving fifty miles away. We can meet up every now and then. And there's the telephone, of course," Tess said, enthusiastically.

Lizzie nodded. "Yes. Perhaps it's meant to be after all."

…

The years passed quickly and with them all the good intentions to stay in touch. Katie soon forgot all about Ben Baker and about boys smelling and being made of worms. She also forgot about never getting married. Though, of course, Katie did have to find a husband-to-be before that could happen.

"So I'm no nearer to needing that special hat for your big day, then?" Lizzie asked, one

weekend when Katie was visiting.

"No and Dad doesn't need to worry about writing that speech, either," Katie agreed, "you're terrible, Mum."

"Well, aren't there any nice young men at the bank I could marry you off to?" Lizzie grinned.

Katie thought about her job. She'd been at the bank for six years, ever since leaving school and she loved it. She'd made friends, gained promotion and the salary had helped her set up home in a quaint little town house. She'd had a couple of boyfriends over the years, but there hadn't been anyone truly special. No one she could imagine spending the rest of her life with.

"You're too fussy, that's your trouble," Lizzie teased.

"I suppose I am. But I'm not going to settle for just anyone, Mum."

"That I do know," Lizzie said, wistfully, "do you remember Ben Baker? He was the son of an old friend. He was a lovely boy, but you took an instant dislike to him."

Katie shuddered. Despite not hearing the name for a very long time, she could remember that awful tongue, remember those hair-pulling hands.

"It's such a shame. Katie Waldron and Ben Baker. It was meant to be, you know," Lizzie said, sighing.

Katie quickly changed the subject.

...

Katie walked into work the Monday morning after with a spring in her step. A new colleague was starting and it was Katie's job to train him. She loved that part of her work best. Meeting new people and helping others was part of the reason Katie had joined the bank.

When Katie reached her desk, someone was already sitting in her place. She didn't recognize the short, dark hair or the soft features. It had to be her new colleague.

"Hello, I'm Katie Waldron," Katie said, holding out her hand.

The handsome face looked into hers. Katie smiled. She hadn't ever been romantically interested in any of her colleagues, but perhaps there was about to be an exception.

"Ben Baker," he replied.

Katie's smile froze. Her hands went hot, then cold.

She stared at Ben. He wasn't sticking his tongue out at her, but away the years fell from his face and there was that horrid little boy again.

"Right, let's get to work," Katie said, abruptly.

If Ben Baker thought she was going to make life easy for him, then he was very much mistaken.

The day dragged like no other day at the bank had ever dragged before. To make matters worse, Ben seemed very pleasant. But it was just a ploy. Just like it had been a ploy all those years ago when he'd been nice and then dropped a spider down her collar.

As Katie trudged home, she started to feel guilty. Ben had looked so confused. He really seemed to have no idea why she was being so standoffish with him and she had to admit, he appeared to be a genuinely nice person.

So why was she being so horrible? Because he was Ben Baker that was why. And because her mother had married her off to him when she was three.

She wanted to choose her own husband, thank you very much. She groaned. She had better not mention anything to her mother about seeing Ben again. That would start all the, 'It's meant to be', again.

The next morning was the first time Katie had dreaded going to work. Perhaps it was time to get a transfer. Maybe it was time to move on.

"Morning, Ben," Katie said, with a big smile. She would be changing offices soon, so she could afford to be pleasant.

"Um, morning," Ben said, sheepishly, clearly hardly daring to speak.

"Look, I'm so sorry about yesterday. I don't know quite how to say it, but we went to pre-school together," Katie blurted out.

"Did we?" Ben said, puzzled.

"Yes. We didn't like each other very much. You poked your tongue out at me and you pulled my hair," Katie couldn't stop herself.

"So that's why you were rude to me yesterday," Ben said, gaining confidence.

"I wasn't rude. Listen to us, we're bickering as if we're back at pre-school," Katie said, laughing despite herself.

"I didn't go to pre-school. My mother's a teacher. She taught me the basics until it was compulsory for me to go to school," Ben said, giving Katie a funny look.

"*Tess wasn't a teacher. She was a dinner lady,*" *Katie hissed.*

"*My mother's name is Eve. I don't even know a Tess,*" *Ben retorted.*

Katie opened her mouth and closed it again. Ben wasn't that unusual a name and Baker was quite a common surname.

"*Oh dear. I think I've been a bit of an idiot,*" *Katie stammered.*

"*Forget about it. Let's start afresh. How about I take you out for a bit of lunch? I promise I won't stick my tongue out at you or pull your hair. Not even once,*" *Ben grinned.*

Katie smiled. Katie Waldron and Ben Baker. Maybe her mother hadn't been so wrong after all. Maybe, just maybe, it was meant to be.

A short story written for a small press magazine:

The Intruder

"*Oh dear, oh dear, oh dear,*" *Tom muttered, staring at his home of the past forty years.*

It wasn't much of a home really; more of a hut, but it was his home. And someone was in it.

He shook his head. He had only been gone twenty minutes. He quite fancied some rabbit for his tea, so he had taken a stroll into the woods. Tom had never been very good at catching things, except coughs and colds, so there he was empty handed and with an intruder in his home.

He took a step forward, cursing as his boots squelched in a muddy puddle. He felt the murky liquid ooze onto his holey socks and snake up between his toes. He grimaced and pushed on, pounding towards home.

Tom stopped outside, his head thumping and a sickness forcing its way into his throat. Hardly a soul had bothered him in all his years there. He grunted as if a fist had flailed him in the stomach. Someone had to own the hut. He was surprised he hadn't been thrown out years before. Where would he go?

He closed his eyes and raw and ragged memories surged into his mind. He had known life on the streets. He wouldn't want it again.

A wail from within the hut pricked at his chest, punching the air from his lungs. Perhaps it was an injured animal, but he was sure there had been a face at the window.

Tom pushed the door and watched as the jagged oak panels effortlessly swung back. This time there was a definite cry – a human cry and one of fear. Feet flew over the stone floor scrambling for safety.

"It's all right. It's only old Tom. I won't hurt you," Tom's gruff voice wasn't the most melodious.

The room wasn't very big and the furniture was sparse, shielding no one. Tom's eyes fell on the young girl huddled by the rickety cupboard in the corner.

"Please, lass, don't be frightened," Tom reached out his hand.

The girl gasped as if touched by a ferocious spark of fire. She pulled back, moulding herself to the wall.

Tom took a step back. The last time he had caught sight of his own reflection, he had scared himself, so it was no wonder the girl was petrified. When he was a lad, he was lucky if he had a bath once a week. Time had only worsened matters and his home boasted no comforts like a bath. He knew his beard needed a trim and if he didn't detangle it soon, he would have birds setting up home in it. His clothes weren't the best either, not that he had ever been one for fashion, but he had seen better on a scarecrow.

Tom walked over to the table taking centre stage. He brushed crumbs and wodges of month-old food from the wood and sat down. He didn't often care about his attire or what others thought of him, but suddenly it mattered.

A smile slowly spread over his face. He pushed himself up and fetched a box from the side. He took out a bun brimming with icing. Rabbit followed by a bun would have made a smashing dinner, but he had no rabbit and now it looked like he would have no bun. His mouth watered and he wished the lady at the park had thrown the other one in the bin as well. But from the way her lips smacked, smearing the icing all round her plump face, he had been fortunate she hadn't scoffed them both.

He held the bun in front of him and trod like a child trying not to spill his drink. He set the bun down on the table and walked towards the door. He paused and forced himself not to look at the girl, before stepping outside.

He stood and witnessed the cool autumn sun begin its descent and the wind whip round his ankles, a warning of the winter to come.

Tom listened to the scurry of feet and the chair scraping back. He wondered whether he should wait. He listened. Silence. He opened the door. The girl couldn't have been any more than fifteen. Chocolate brown eyes gazed up at him from behind an overgrown fringe of mousy hair.

"Go on, that's it. Enjoy the cake," Tom said, moving forward with each word. "You're a run away, aren't you, lass?"

The girl looked ready for flight.

"No, lass, don't go. I understand. You see I'm a runaway, too."

The brown eyes searched his face and she frowned, but her shoulders relaxed a little. Tom pulled out the other chair and looked to the girl for approval. She nodded, though still wary of her host.

Tom sighed and as words tumbled from his mouth, the years fell away. He was ten years old again. The war had ended. England was victorious and people were dancing in the streets. But not Tom.

His Aunt Ethel stood in front of him and a shroud of darkness hung over her from head to toe. His father always said his mother's sister was a witch. It was their secret. His father would tuck him into bed every night and they would tell each other stories about Aunt Ethel and her broomstick. But Tom hadn't wanted to laugh any more. Not now his mother and father were dead, taken away by the cruelness of war. Not now he would be moving to Scotland for a new life with Aunt Ethel.

Tom had soon found out she wasn't a witch. He wished she had been. After the passing of sixty years, the physical scars had vanished, but the mental ones would always remain. Tom's mind and body could bear no more and he had run until he could run no longer. Street-life had not come easy to the young lad, but he had turned his hand to anything and he soon began to make a life for himself. The years passed and with them the shedding of childhood and the emergence of a man. Lucy had come along and Tom felt happiness beckon.

As Tom retold his tale, tears came to his eyes as he remembered John, the loan shark. Tom never forgave himself for borrowing the money in the first place and when they took his Lucy, his life was over.

"You ran again, didn't you?" the young girl interrupted his reminiscence.

"I did indeed, lass. I went running for years until I found this place and here I've stayed. What for, I don't know. I don't know," Tom whispered, his body shaking with sobs.

A hand covered his. Tom almost recoiled from the contact. It was so long since he had felt another's touch. He looked up at the girl and felt her warmth spread throughout him. Her eyes glistened with tears.

"So what's made you run away, lass?" Tom snorted, drying his eyes with an old rag.

"Nothing like what you've been through," the girl started sheepishly.

"Come now, something's made you run."

She nodded and patted her stomach. Tom's eyes followed, taking in the expanding waistline.

"Your lad left you as well, eh?"

Again, the nod.

"I failed my exams, too," she said, giving in to a further flurry of tears.

"You're in a bit of a pickle there, but it's not all bad. I bet your mum and dad are worried about you. Expect they'd give anything to have you back home. What's your name, lass?"

"Bethany. As mums and dads go, they're great, but they'll kill me for this," she couldn't go on.

"I doubt that. I doubt that very much. Of course they'll be mad at first, but you're their daughter. They'll help you through it all, every step of the way, lass. You've got to go back to them. Don't end up like me."

Bethany squeezed Tom's hand. Neither needed to speak.

Darkness had descended and caught them unawares. Tom walked over to the ancient gas fire. One day he knew it wouldn't turn, but it had been one of his most faithful friends. He made a sumptuous supper of beans on toast and the two talked until the early hours of the morning like age-old friends.

Sunlight stabbed his eyes and Tom roused himself from a peaceful sleep. He hoped Bethany didn't mind beans on toast again. Perhaps he would push the boat out and go and get some eggs. Old Farmer Joe was good to him.

Tom glanced round the room. He was alone. He pushed himself to his feet and found the note on the table.

Dear Tom,

I rang Mum on my mobile. She cried and asked me to come home. She said she loved me and she would be there for me whatever I've done.

Thank you, Tom. I'll always remember you. You are an angel sent from heaven.

Lots of love,

Bethany

'Drat,' Tom said, knowing he was going to cry and trying to find his rag. Though, for some reason, he couldn't help but smile. Maybe it was because he had his home back to himself again, but he rather thought it was for another reason.

A short story written for an anthology of flash fiction:

First Sight

The stench hit his nostrils. He was going to be sick, but it wasn't anything to do with the smell. His palms were sweating and he couldn't stop shaking.

Shouts were gaining, a crowd chanting louder and louder. A roar pierced the air close by. The stale bread and filthy water he had eaten for breakfast flew from his mouth. Hands grabbed him, jagged nails digging into flesh.

Darkness, deeper and deeper, dragging him down. He smiled, snaking his way towards it. They wouldn't let him and yanked him to his feet, kicking him in the ribs, the back and legs.

Sunlight stabbed him as he was thrown outside. A sea of eyes stared down at him, mocking and jeering at him.

For a moment, he didn't care, unable to take his gaze from the magnificent sight. He hadn't believed them, but every word was true. It was the first time he had seen the Coliseum. The tiger pounced, ensuring it was his last.

'First Sight' is a flash fiction story. Flash fiction is sometimes referred to as mini-stories or micro-stories. It can be anything from a few words, up to 1000 words. Typical flash fiction tends to be either 100, 250 or 500 words.

A short story written for a children's ezine:

Clarissa's Cake

It was Clarissa's birthday. Clarissa wanted a birthday cake. And not just any birthday cake.

"I want a big birthday cake," Clarissa said. "The biggest birthday cake in the world."

Clarissa and her mummy walked round and round the cake shop in search of the best big birthday cake.

"What about this one?" Clarissa's mummy said.

Clarissa looked at the cake. It was big, with pink and purple icing dripping down over a soft sponge.

"No, I want a bigger cake," Clarissa said, sulking.

Clarissa's mummy sighed. "What about this one?" she said, pointing to a bigger cake.

The cake was yellow, with yummy sugary sweets on top.

"No, I want a much bigger cake," Clarissa said, stamping her feet.

Clarissa's mummy frowned. "What about this one?" she said, finding a much bigger cake.

The cake was a terrific triangle shape in magnificent mauve with marshmallows clinging to the sides.

"No, I want an even bigger cake," Clarissa said, sucking her thumb and twiddling her hair.

Clarissa's mummy walked to the back of the cake shop. Clarissa's mummy didn't sigh. Clarissa's mummy didn't frown. For Clarissa's mummy had found an even bigger cake.

"What about this one?" she said, pointing to the biggest cake in the world.

Clarissa and her mummy looked up and up and up. They looked up as far as they could see and still the cake went up and up.

"Yes, I want that cake," Clarissa said, smiling and jumping up and down.

The cake seemed to shimmer and change colour.

"Yummy," Clarissa said, "look, it's changed into a chocolate cake now."

The shopkeeper winked at Clarissa's mummy. And Clarissa's mummy winked back.

"Look, now it's an orange cake. It's changed again. It's a lemon cake now," Clarissa said, squirming with excitement.

"Would you like to try some?" the shopkeeper asked.

"Yes, I want some now," Clarissa said, snatching a huge handful of cake.

Clarissa tipped her head back and opened her mouth very, very wide. Then she gulped the cake down in one go.

"Ugh!" Clarissa said, screwing up her face, "it's horrible. It tastes like grass. No, it tastes like mud. No, now it tastes like worms."

Clarissa chomped and chewed. But the more she chomped and chewed the more horrible the flavours became.

"Perhaps you would prefer this cake?" the shopkeeper said.

Clarissa looked at the cake in the shopkeeper's hands. It was small and round and covered in white icing. The words, 'Happy Birthday' were printed in rainbow letters on the top and pretty ponies and flowers circled the words.

Clarissa nodded. It was perfect.

"Thank you very much," Clarissa said.

As she said the words, the biggest cake in the world disappeared and so did the terrible taste in Clarissa's mouth.

Clarissa clutched her birthday cake in one hand and her mummy's hand in the other. And together they went home.

Competition-winning Stories

A short story, which won an international short story competition:

A Special Friend

I didn't know what had happened. Not at first. And then I knew. I didn't hurt any more.

It was wonderful. I had always hurt. I couldn't remember a time when I didn't hurt. But there must have been a time. Once. Before the beatings began. Before Mummy and Daddy died.

I can't remember my mummy and daddy. They look nice in the photographs, but everybody looks nice in photographs. Even Aunt Maud and Uncle Frank look nice in photographs. They look very old. As Aunt Maud kept telling me, Mummy was a mistake. Granny Violet had wanted to 'get rid of her' because she didn't want to have any more children, but the doctors said she was too late. I'm glad she was too late.

I don't mind old people. Father Christmas is old. He didn't ever come to Aunt Maud and Uncle Frank's house, but he came to school once. I wanted to go with him when he left. I thought I could go and help him with the reindeer. I told Father Christmas I could help to make all the toys, too, and fly with him around the world on Christmas Eve. He laughed and ruffled my hair. How I wished I could have gone with him.

Aunt Maud and Uncle Frank were nice at first. They didn't have children of their own. They hadn't been 'blessed' with them, they said. They told me I was a 'gift from God', that He had taken away my parents so their lives were complete.

And then they changed. It was Aunt Maud at first. I was getting ready for school one morning and my nail went through my tights. I laughed and went to get another pair. There weren't any in the drawer. When I asked Aunt Maud if she had any more, she struck me to the ground. It hurt. How it hurt. I remember turning to her and looking up at her, waiting for her to say she was sorry, that she didn't know what had come over her.

Perhaps she would hug me to her and kiss my head. She didn't. She stood there, with her hand on her hip and her foot tapping. Her face was red and her lips white where her teeth were chomping down on them. My eyes went up to her nose and the nostrils, narrow one minute and wide the next. Up my eyes went to hers, usually so clear and blue but cloudy and cold then. I had seen books with pictures of werewolves, vampires and all sorts of creatures on them. I had thought they were stories. I wasn't so sure any more.

Aunt Maud opened her mouth then, that very wide mouth, hidden most of the time by thin, chapped lips. I was certain she was going to eat me whole.

"You evil child. The bible tells of children born of the devil, Lucy. I always detested your mother. Right from the moment she was born. I rejoiced when she died. And that no-hoper father of yours. Then I thought we had been given a chance to put right a wrong. But you're just like them. You must be punished. The bible insists upon it." I was sure the words flew from her mouth.

They were words I never forgot. They weren't the last either.

Uncle Frank wasn't so bad, but Aunt Maud lied. She told him about things I hadn't done. She told him I was wicked and that I did terrible things to her. He believed her. Then he would come to me and beat me. He was so big, so strong, so powerful. Afterwards, he told me not to cry and said he was sorry. He hugged me and his own tears joined mine. As quickly as they had come, those tears dried when Aunt Maud came to inspect his work.

School was the only place where I could get away. I loved school. The teachers talked about what wonderful things I could do when I grew up. Policemen and nurses came to school to talk about their jobs. The teachers told me I could be anything I wanted to be as long as I worked hard. I learnt about foreign countries and lands far, far away. I made friends, too.

I thought Aunt Maud would be pleased. I thought she would want me to do well, to be good and to be liked by the teachers and children. She didn't and she tried to take me away from school. Said I had to stay home with her. She made me cook and clean. Told me she would teach me all I needed to know. She said I had been getting above my station, that I was too stupid to learn and to make something of myself. She told me I wouldn't ever go to school again.

But she couldn't do that. The school kept ringing and then they came round. I thought about telling them everything. Maybe they would take me away and I could go and live with someone nice who didn't hurt me.

Aunt Maud was so nice to them. She made them lots of tea and brought them her best biscuits. They liked Aunt Maud. They believed every word she said.

At least it meant I could go back to school. There was nothing Aunt Maud could do. It was the law.

"But don't go getting any grand ideas. You're nothing. You're worthless. And I don't want to hear about any friends, either. I've put the school right about you, young lady. I told them what a wicked child you are and how they don't see what you're really like."

Her words worked. Everyone was different towards me when I went back to school. All I wanted was a friend. Just one special friend. But I had no one.

...

I had often thought about ghosts. I'm sure every child thinks about ghosts. I wasn't sure I believed in them, but when you become one, you have to. It was a bit strange, seeing my body, so small, so stiff, there in Uncle Frank's arms.

"What have you done? What have you done, woman?" he shouted at Aunt Maud.

It all went a bit mad then. Uncle Frank lost it. Aunt Maud went purple before Uncle Frank let go of her neck. I was glad he did. She wouldn't have made a very nice ghost.

Then the sirens started. People came running in. Policemen. Ambulance men. Voices shouted. People prodded and poked at my body. Aunt Maud was quiet, so very quiet. Her body was still, like one of the stuffed teddies I had until Aunt Maud threw them out. Uncle Frank just sobbed, shaking with hulking great tears.

"Why? Why didn't I stop her? I knew. I knew what she was doing. I knew she'd go too far one day. I failed you, Lucy," he said, over and over and then he ran to my body and lay protectively across it.

I think Uncle Frank will make a nice ghost one day.

I didn't know what to do then. I didn't want to stay there any more. But I didn't know where to go. I felt something tug me. I wondered if I was going up to heaven. All little girls and boys went up to heaven, apart from me. I wasn't nice. I wasn't as bad as Aunt Maud said I was. I was certain of that, but I had to be a little bit bad, otherwise she wouldn't have hurt me.

I wasn't tugged upwards, so I knew I wasn't going to heaven. I wasn't tugged down either so I wasn't going to that other horrible place. Instead, I was tugged sideways, right through the wall and out, away from Aunt Maud and Uncle Frank. I was pulled further, across hills and hedges, fields and forests. I didn't want to stop. I felt free, flying away from everything.

And then the tugging stopped. Just like that. I didn't see him to start with. He was only little. Like me. He was crying. He looked so lost, so sad just sat there on a small stone wall outside a little house. I wanted to hug him and to tell him everything would be all right.

But I couldn't. I would have frightened him if I had done that. My arm would probably have gone right through him and then he would really have started to cry. And scream. People would have come running and I'd probably have been reported to the Ghost Council or whatever it was called. They might have made me go back to Aunt Maud.

Something shiny caught my eye. It was a ball. A bright blue ball. I pushed it along the ground towards the boy and turned away. I had to go. I couldn't help him. Then I looked back. I don't know why I did. The boy was looking straight at me.

I waited for the scream. It didn't come. Instead, he pushed the ball back to me, his tears slowing.

"Can you see me?" I asked.

"You're a ghost. Of course I can see you," he said.

"How do you know?"

"Because I'm a ghost, too. I don't want to be a ghost," he said and started to cry harder.

I did hug him then. And he hugged me back. It felt so good to be hugged. He couldn't stop crying and then I found neither could I. We didn't stop crying for ages.

His name's Sam. He had a lovely mummy and daddy. A brother and sister, too. He didn't want to die, but the Leukaemia took over. We've taken it one day at a time, little by little and Sam doesn't cry so much now.

When I first saw him, I wondered if I had been sent to help others. Now I know I have. There's a little girl who's been in an accident and who looks very unsure. Sam was my first friend. My first special friend. Now I know there's going to be many more.

A flash fiction story, which won a competition in one of the women's weeklies:

Sally knew the woman was going to hurt her. She thought about running away, but the woman stood between her and the door. The woman smiled. Sally was sure there was a glint in her eye; she clearly loved to torture her victims.

Sally took a deep breath. She mustn't cry. Had all the others? She jumped as she felt the heat, sure it was scorching her skin. She closed her eyes, gasping at the pain. She had to be near the end now.

One thing was certain - she was never having a bikini wax again.

Note: A title wasn't required for the above story, but this is an exception to the norm. If you're in any doubt, always check the rules.

A flash fiction story, which won a small press competition:

Waiting

George was going to die. His weather-beaten face was going through the whole spectrum of Teletubbies: yellow, green, red and finally purple. His bushy brows furrowed then did a little pirouette to see how high they could go. His lips quivered, twitching before his false teeth clamped down on them. This was awful. He couldn't take much more.

It was late September, but for some reason the string vest and best beige shorts felt like a fur coat. He clutched his chest, feeling its beat building to a crescendo like a volcano waiting to spill piping hot lava onto the unsuspecting hoards below.

He thought of Sheila. He had to fight it. He couldn't let her see him like this. He took a deep breath, gagging as a fly looped the loop into his mouth.

Specks of spittle gathered at the side of his lips as the fly's wings tickled his tongue. As George opened wide and the fly spluttered to the floor, he heard the kitchen door open. It was Sheila. She'd come.

George wiped his eyes. It wasn't supposed to be like this. The day had started so well, but this was the moment he had been waiting for. But what if Sheila ruined it? And she could so easily. Perhaps she didn't care any more. Maybe she no longer loved him.

George stared at his sandals. They were lovely sandals, though the white socks probably didn't show them off to their best. Neither did the earwig staggering across them. George thought about flicking it off. He couldn't move. If he moved, he would have to face Sheila.

He could feel her eyes boring into him. At least she had come. That had to mean something, surely?

His nostrils took on a life of their own. He could smell something. It was probably nothing. His hearing aid screeched in his ear. People were gathering, crowding round him. Voices chanting, breaths on his face.

His eyes blurred, a mist of tears hanging over them. This was it. He dared to look.

The crowd parted and Sheila stood before him. Her beautiful face lit up the room as she walked towards him. There was something in her hands. Could it be?

It wasn't. The choke caught in his throat and he fought for breath. His head pounded and the room was spinning.

"Come on, let's get you sat down," Sheila said, smoothing everything over as always, "look what I've got. It's come."

He shoved the envelope aside, "Don't want it."

"All right, all right. I remembered. You and your chocolate cake," Sheila said, fetching the huge mountain of sponge from the kitchen.

George felt the tears roll down his cheek, though this time they were for a different reason.

'To the best dad in the World. Happy 100th birthday', he read the words on the cake.

Shouts and clapping filled the room. George looked at the envelope. He supposed he had better see what the Queen had to say.

A short story, which won a writing magazine competition:

The Final Journey

I can't stand this. This is the worst journey of my entire life. I think I'm going to be sick. I wind the car window down and feel the short, sharp blast of early morning air. That's better. Stomach back under control. But I'm not. Now I'm going to cry.

I blink back the tears and look out the smeary window. A hint of blue tries its best to lighten the leaden-looking clouds. It doesn't succeed. Cows graze on grass, their mouths moving slowly, oblivious to the pricks of rain patting their skin.

I look away and find my eyes locking with a pair of brown eyes, eyes I have seen far too much of over the past fortnight. Sandy, as she insisted I call her, reaches across and takes my hand.

"It's all right. Not long now," she says.

I pull my hand away. But what if it isn't all right? What if she's wrong? What if it's never all right ever again?

I think back to when I first met her — on that Monday afternoon two weeks ago.

"Hello, Mrs Martin, I'm Sandy," she said.

Sarah, Samantha, Sandy; it was all the same to me. I didn't care. I didn't care about anything at all. Only Kim. Kim was my world. Always had been, always would be, especially so since her dad, my husband, had died two years ago. We had clung to each other and helped each other get through. We were so close. I had thought nothing would ever come between us — until that Monday.

It had begun like any other week — frantically. Neither of us were morning people and that Monday we had overslept. The supervisor at the office had retired and the new one was intent on imposing her mark. Lateness was not something she tolerated. Things were going from bad to worse when Kim spilt her cornflakes and milk everywhere.

"Great! Another thing for me to clear up. Why can't you be more careful?" I had shouted.

Kim didn't say anything. She just slammed the door and stomped off to school. I never saw her again. Why did I shout at her? She could have covered the whole house in cornflakes and milk and it wouldn't have mattered. I could have been given the sack and that wouldn't have mattered either. Nothing mattered except my darling daughter.

I should have told her I loved her, that she meant the world to me and I never wanted to be without her whatever happened. But I didn't. I didn't say it.

The car stops. I look out the window. More cows. In the road this time. One stands right in front of the car. The driver hoots the horn. The cow continues its saunter across the road. Another one takes its place and decides to take a break from his journey. The horn is honked again and a fist shaken at the cow.

"It's really going to take notice of that, isn't it? What on Earth did you do that for?" Sandy says, jabbing a long, bony finger into the driver's neck.

I remember saying almost the same thing to Sandy. It was the Wednesday by then. Forty-eight hours after Kim had gone missing.

"What on Earth did she do that for? She never misses school and she certainly knows not to get into a stranger's car. It can't have been her," I had almost pleaded with Sandy.

But it was her. On the CCTV footage. 8.45 Monday 7th March when she should have been walking through the school gates. Instead she had been climbing into a battered old Ford Mondeo.

"Perhaps it wasn't a stranger. Perhaps she knew the driver," Sandy had suggested, ever so politely.

I hated her then. Hated Sandy with her sleekly styled hair and carefully made-up face. I hated the soft, silky voice I was sure every man loved. I hated her for her youth, her childless world. What did she know? What gave her the right to make assumptions about my daughter? I knew my daughter. Sandy didn't. She knew nothing about her.

I can feel Sandy looking at me as the car jolts into action once more leaving behind all the cows in their new grazing ground. I turn to her. See her smile. See her care. See beyond the pristine and perfect face she presents to the world.

I smile, too. She reaches out her hand and this time I squeeze it. Hold it. She feels my pain and I feel hers. I think about the things she has told me, things many of her colleagues don't know. About her sister. The twin she thought she knew so well but didn't know at all. Not until she was murdered by one of the clients she rented her body out to.

I couldn't hate Sandy then and yet I knew what she was implying. That I didn't know my own daughter. That perhaps we don't really know anyone. But I did know my daughter. Of course I did. Just because her sister had led a double life didn't mean my daughter did. My daughter wouldn't know anyone with a dented old car. She didn't like boys and certainly not boys old enough to drive. Yes, she had started to stay round her friends' houses and become more independent. She was nearly fifteen, beginning the gradual journey of leaving childhood and becoming a woman.

But she was still my little girl. I had felt her grow inside me and kick me with those tiny feet. I had given birth to her and nurtured her over the years. I knew everything about her.

But I didn't. Sandy was right. I didn't know about the boyfriend. The older man. Much older. I didn't know about the criminal record. GBH. Theft. Armed robbery. Sandy said his name was Ray. Friends gradually came forward and told the police how Kim had been seeing Ray for a few months. Ray's acquaintances were questioned. More of his sordid life was revealed.

The happy, fun-loving, carefree daughter I saw every day wasn't the one everyone else knew. She had been. Oh yes, up until two years ago. I thought she had coped. I thought we had helped one another through the bad times. She had coped with her father's death so much better than I. But she hadn't, not really. Things affect us all in different ways.

I am still looking at Sandy. She is staring ahead. I wonder if she is thinking about her journey. The final one to identify her sister's body. I shudder and feel the tears threaten again. She didn't tell me about it. She didn't want to go that far — for me or for her. But there was no one else. Mother, father and brother had all died in a car crash when she and her sister were in their late teens. How can I have thought she didn't understand? How could I have hated her?

Her head turns. She touches my shoulder. I wonder what made her tell me. What connected her to me. Maybe it was seeing the shock on my face when she told me about Ray. My face had crumpled. I know it had. Along with my whole world. She must have seen that same look plenty of times. On other mothers' faces. And yet she hadn't told them. Stay impartial, don't get too close. It's just a job.

Perhaps I reminded her of her sister. The sister she thought she knew. Sandy feels like a sister to me. A friend, too. A friend when no one else can find the right words to say. A friend who understands every heart-breaking moment you are going through and knows that every breath you take hurts each and every part of your body. A friend whose bond with you will never break. When something so bad, so appalling happens, how can something good emerge? Life does that.

I think about Kim when she was small. She loved her bedtime story. She always chose the stories about witches and monsters. No Cinderella or Prince Charming for her. She turned her nose up at fairy tales. I laughed, so convinced she would meet her prince one day and I would watch her glide down the aisle in a flowing dress.

Maybe she will. I didn't think the phone call would ever come. She didn't speak at first. But I knew it was Kim. I couldn't speak either.

"Mum? Mum!"

"Kim!" I was shaking so much I could barely hold the receiver.

"I want to come home. I've made such a stupid mistake. I'm sorry, Mum, so sorry."

I had dreamt about hearing those words over and over. Deep down, I had thought a dream is all they would ever be.

Sandy's tearful eyes had mirrored my own and then she had taken over. Told me what to say, made phone calls and plans. Ray was apprehended. Kim taken to hospital. They said she was fine, but I wouldn't know that until I saw her. And I will see her in about five minutes. I can see the hospital in the distance.

What shall I do when I see her? Hug her? Tell her off?

The car has stopped now. I can see a sign for reception. I look at Sandy. My journey is ending so differently to hers. Did she think mine would be the same? Is that why she told me? She smiles, such a warm, happy smile. I know the answer.

I ask the way at reception and step into the lift. The doors close and I am carried upwards, the final stage of my journey. When the door opens, a new one will begin. It won't be easy. There will be lots of tears and talking. Hard times but hopefully plenty of good. At least I know where to start. I'll tell her I love her, that she means the world to me and I never want to be without her – whatever happens.

Useful Information

Resources for writers

There are lots of magazines and books for writers. Here are some well-known ones, which have been offering help to writers for years:

Writers' and Artists' Yearbook
published annually. https://www.writersandartists.co.uk

Writing Magazine
published monthly. https://www.writers-online.co.uk

Writers' Forum
published monthly. https://writers-forum.com

Courses

You'll find a wide variety of places offering courses for writers, from universities, to magazines, to the Internet. The few detailed here have been tried and tested for years:

The Writers Bureau
distance learning courses for writers, ranging from article and short story writing, to novel writing and writing for competitions.
https://www.writersbureau.com

Arvon

residential writing courses, covering a diverse range of genres, from poetry and fiction, to screenwriting and comedy.
https://www.arvon.org

Swanwick Summer School

week-long summer school, featuring all sorts of courses and workshops, from writing fillers, to advice on photography, to writing for magazines.
https://www.swanwickwritersschool.org.uk

Writing Festivals

There are a plethora of literary and writing festivals to attend throughout the year. Some feature talks by well-known writers while others run workshops to help writers learn. A few offer a mixture of both. Here are some of interest:

Stratford Literary Festival.
http://www.stratfordliteraryfestival.co.uk

The Charleston Festival.
https://www.charleston.org.uk/festival/about-the-charleston-festival/

Theakston Old Peculiar Crime Writing Festival,
Harrogate.
https://harrogateinternationalfestivals.com/crime-writing-festival/

Indie Fest, Bradford.
https://www.indiefestuk.com

Henley Literary Festival.
http://www.henleyliteraryfestival.co.uk

Cheltenham Festival of Literature.
https://www.cheltenhamfestivals.com/literature/

ABOUT THE AUTHOR

Esther Chilton has always loved words and writing, but she started out working with figures in a bank. She was on an accelerated training programme and studying banking exams, which meant she didn't have time for writing, so it wasn't long before it was a thing of the past – or so she thought. Her love affair with writing ignited again when she had a serious injury to her back. It meant she could no longer carry out her job working in the bank and it led her back to writing, which has become a daily part of her life.

She has now been working as a freelance writer for over twenty years, regularly writing articles and short stories for magazines and newspapers such as *Freelance Market News, Writers' Forum, Writing Magazine, The Guardian, Best of British, The Cat, This England* and *The People's Friend* to name a few.

Winner of several competitions, including those run by *Writing Magazine and Writers' News,* Esther has also had the privilege of judging writing competitions.

As well as working as a freelance writer, she has branched out into the exciting world of copywriting, providing copy for sales letters, brochures, leaflets, web pages, slogans and emails.

Esther loves writing but equally she enjoys helping others, which she achieves in her role as a tutor for The *Writers Bureau.* She feels like a proud parent when one of her students has a piece of writing published. Some of them have gone on to become published authors and have achieved great success.

In addition to tutoring, Esther works as a freelance copyeditor offering an editing, guidance and advice service for authors and writers. She has edited novels, non-fiction books, articles and short stories. You can find out more about it here: https://esthernewtonblog.wordpress.com/editing-proofreading-and-advice-service/

If you'd like Esther's help, or would like to know more about what she can do for you, please get in touch: **estherchilton@gmail.com**

Other links:

- **Blog**: https://esthernewtonblog.wordpress.com

- **Twitter**: Esther Chilton @esthernewton201

- **Facebook**: https://www.facebook.com/esther.chilton1

- **Linkedin**: Esther Chilton

YOUR NOTES

PUBLICATION GUARANTEED (Well, almost!)

PUBLICATION GUARANTEED (Well, almost!)

PUBLICATION GUARANTEED (Well, almost!)

Printed in Great Britain
by Amazon

34749776R00097